Current
CONTROVERSIES

Homeland Security

Other Books in the Current Controversies Series

Homeland Security

Debra A. Miller, Book Editor

GREENHAVEN PRESS
A part of Gale, Cengage Learning

GALE
CENGAGE Learning

Detroit • New York • San Francisco • New Haven, Conn • Waterville, Maine • London

Christine Nasso, *Publisher*
Elizabeth Des Chenes, *Managing Editor*

© 2009 Greenhaven Press, a part of Gale, Cengage Learning

Gale and Greenhaven Press are registered trademarks used herein under license.

For more information, contact:
Greenhaven Press
27500 Drake Rd.
Farmington Hills, MI 48331-3535
Or you can visit our Internet site at gale.cengage.com

For product information and technology assistance, contact us at

Gale Customer Support, 1-800-877-4253
For permission to use material from this text or product, submit all requests online at
www.cengage.com/permissions

Further permissions questions can be emailed to permissionrequest@cengage.com

Articles in Greenhaven Press anthologies are often edited for length to meet page requirements. In addition, original titles of these works are changed to clearly present the main thesis and to explicitly indicate the author's opinion. Every effort is made to ensure that Greenhaven Press accurately reflects the original intent of the authors. Every effort has been made to trace the owners of copyrighted material.

Cover image copyright James Steidl, 2008. Used under license from Shutterstock.com.

LIBRARY OF CONGRESS CATALOGING-IN-PUBLICATION DATA

Homeland security / Debra A. Miller, book editor.
    p. cm. -- (Current controversies)
    Includes bibliographical references and index.
    ISBN-13: 978-0-7377-4138-4 (hardcover)
    ISBN-13: 978-0-7377-4139-1 (pbk.)
    1. United States. Dept. of Homeland Security. 2. Terrorism--United States-- Prevention. 3. Internal security--United States. 4. National security--United States. 5. Civil rights--United States. I. I. Miller, Debra A.
    HV6432.4.H65 2009
    363.325'15610973--dc22
                                   2008016191

Printed in the United States of America
2 3 4 5 6   14 13 12 11 10

ED133

Contents

Chapter 3: What Measures Should Be Taken to Enhance Homeland Security?

Chapter 4: Do Efforts to Enhance Homeland Security Threaten Civil Liberties?

No: Efforts to Enhance Homeland Security Do Not Threaten Civil Liberties

Foreword

By definition, controversies are "discussions of questions in which opposing opinions clash" (Webster's Twentieth Century Dictionary Unabridged). Few would deny that controversies are a pervasive part of the human condition and exist on virtually every level of human enterprise. Controversies transpire between individuals and among groups, within nations and between nations. Controversies supply the grist necessary for progress by providing challenges and challengers to the status quo. They also create atmospheres where strife and warfare can flourish. A world without controversies would be a peaceful world; but it also would be, by and large, static and prosaic.

The Series' Purpose

The purpose of the *Current Controversies* series is to explore many of the social, political, and economic controversies dominating the national and international scenes today. Titles selected for inclusion in the series are highly focused and specific. For example, from the larger category of criminal justice, *Current Controversies* deals with specific topics such as police brutality, gun control, white collar crime, and others. The debates in *Current Controversies* also are presented in a useful, timeless fashion. Articles and book excerpts included in each title are selected if they contribute valuable, long-range ideas to the overall debate. And wherever possible, current information is enhanced with historical documents and other relevant materials. Thus, while individual titles are current in focus, every effort is made to ensure that they will not become quickly outdated. Books in the *Current Controversies* series will remain important resources for librarians, teachers, and students for many years.

In addition to keeping the titles focused and specific, great care is taken in the editorial format of each book in the series. Book introductions and chapter prefaces are offered to provide background material for readers. Chapters are organized around several key questions that are answered with diverse opinions representing all points on the political spectrum. Materials in each chapter include opinions in which authors clearly disagree as well as alternative opinions in which authors may agree on a broader issue but disagree on the possible solutions. In this way, the content of each volume in *Current Controversies* mirrors the mosaic of opinions encountered in society. Readers will quickly realize that there are many viable answers to these complex issues. By questioning each author's conclusions, students and casual readers can begin to develop the critical thinking skills so important to evaluating opinionated material.

Current Controversies is also ideal for controlled research. Each anthology in the series is composed of primary sources taken from a wide gamut of informational categories including periodicals, newspapers, books, U.S. and foreign government documents, and the publications of private and public organizations. Readers will find factual support for reports, debates, and research papers covering all areas of important issues. In addition, an annotated table of contents, an index, a book and periodical bibliography, and a list of organizations to contact are included in each book to expedite further research.

Perhaps more than ever before in history, people are confronted with diverse and contradictory information. During the Persian Gulf War, for example, the public was not only treated to minute-to-minute coverage of the war, it was also inundated with critiques of the coverage and countless analyses of the factors motivating U.S. involvement. Being able to sort through the plethora of opinions accompanying today's major issues, and to draw one's own conclusions, can be a complicated and frustrating struggle. It is the editors' hope that *Current Controversies* will help readers with this struggle.

Introduction

"Since [9/11], the United States has spent hundreds of billions of taxpayer dollars, all in the name of fighting terrorism and increasing homeland security."

Al Qaeda's September 11, 2001, terrorist attacks on the United States changed American attitudes about terrorism and led to dramatic and expensive changes for U.S. security. The attacks, which struck the U.S. homeland, made many Americans feel afraid and unprotected. Government officials responded with a multitude of military, legislative, and policy initiatives designed to counter the terrorist threat and improve national security. The new U.S. "war on terror" began just days after the attacks, on September 20, 2001, when U.S. President George W. Bush spoke to the nation and promised to use every resource and tool to disrupt and defeat the global terror network. Since that time, the United States has spent hundreds of billions of taxpayer dollars, all in the name of fighting terrorism and increasing homeland security.

The first volleys in the war on terror were major military actions. Less than a month after the 9/11 attacks, on October 7, 2001, the United States attacked Afghanistan's Taliban government, which it accused of harboring al Qaeda terrorists. In short order, U.S. troops destroyed al Qaeda bases in Afghanistan, ousted the pro-al Qaeda Taliban government, and ran al Qaeda leaders out of the country. Next, in March 2003, the Bush administration expanded the war on terror to Iraq, a country that administration officials claimed was trying to develop weapons of mass destruction (WMD)—chemical, biological, and nuclear weapons. Although no clear link was ever established between Iraq and the attacks on 9/11, U.S. troops invaded the country and quickly overthrew the regime of

Iraqi dictator Saddam Hussein. As years passed, however, the Iraq war dragged on because of the lack of a stable Iraqi government, a rising anti-government insurgency, and the growth of al Qaeda terrorism in the country. Insecurity and conflict also persists today in Afghanistan where the Taliban are trying to regroup. As a result, more than five years later, U.S. troops are still fighting in both Iraq and Afghanistan—at an ever-increasing price. According to a 2007 report from the Congressional Research Service, a nonpartisan group that provides advice to the U.S. Congress, the tab for these military efforts is expected to reach $758 billion in fiscal year 2008. Furthermore, even if many U.S. troops are eventually withdrawn, experts say the total taxpayer bill for operations in both countries could be between $1 trillion and $1.45 trillion by 2017.

Along with these foreign military efforts, the U.S. government initiated a series of domestic counter-terrorism measures. As a first step, Congress passed the 2001 Aviation and Transportation Security Act, which established the Transportation Security Administration (TSA) and led the government to spend billions on high-technology equipment to screen baggage for weapons and bombs at airports, harbors, and federal sites. Additional monies were spent on other aspects of transportation security—to hire a new workforce of airport screeners; retrofit aircraft with anti-terrorist devices; train armed air marshals to ride along on random flights; and secure federal buildings, seaports, and borders. The total cost of these programs has been estimated at more than $41 billion.

In 2002, the government also created a huge new federal department, called the Department of Homeland Security (DHS), to oversee the various domestic anti-terrorist programs. Since then, the department has spent large sums of money and its budget has grown substantially each year. In fiscal year 2000, for example, the United States spent only $13 billion on homeland security, but the Department of Homeland Security's budget for 2007 was $42.99 billion, an increase of more than 300 percent. For 2008, the department budget was approved at $47.02 billion, a nine percent increase over the previous year. Many DHS grants were made to states to help them beef up first-responder forces (such as police, paramedics, and firefighters), but in many cases, federal funding was insufficient and states and localities were forced to spend significant portions of their own budgets on enhancing security for public sites, events, and potential terrorist targets.

Many experts argue that some of the heaviest costs of the war on terror, however, are nonmonetary costs. For example, a number of terrorism authorities believe that the U.S. military excursion into Iraq soured American relations with other countries, created deep resentment against the United States in the Muslim world, and produced more international terrorism. Although the Bush administration denies that the Iraq war has increased terrorism and claims that fighting terrorists in Iraq prevents them from coming to America, critics point out that the Iraq region now produces more suicide bombings than anywhere else on the globe.

Another consequence of the U.S. war on terror, according to civil liberties advocates, is a threat to individual freedoms enshrined in the U.S. Constitution. Critics say that several Bush administration initiatives have vastly expanded the government's search, surveillance, and interrogation powers at the expense of Americans' constitutional rights to free speech and privacy. Almost immediately after 9/11, for example, President Bush proposed new legislation called the USA PATRIOT Act (Uniting and Strengthening America by Providing Appropriate Tools Required to Intercept and Obstruct Terrorism), which critics saw as a huge expansion of the government's power to conduct searches of Americans' private property and information. For example, the law allows the Federal Bureau of Investigation (FBI) to search private homes and property in secret, permits taps on people's phones and monitoring of their Internet communications, and authorizes law enforcement to search a wide variety of personal financial and other records. The law was reauthorized in 2006 with some civil rights safeguards, but many of these new searches and surveillances are still permitted, most without any type of advance judicial warrant or oversight.

President Bush also took other post-9/11 actions that sparked civil rights complaints. In 2002, the president authorized the National Security Agency, a government intelligence agency charged with collecting information on foreigners, to monitor millions of U.S. telephone calls without the court search warrants normally required for domestic spying. In August 2007, Congress voted to uphold this NSA surveillance program, using techniques known as "data mining," with the passage of the Protect America Act. Additional actions taken by the administration in the name of 9/11 include the prolonged detention of nearly five hundred terrorist suspects in a U.S. military base in Guantánamo, Cuba, without charging them with a crime. The administration also defends certain interrogation techniques in terror investigations that some consider to be torture. Many experts see these decisions as violations of both the U.S. Constitution and the Geneva Conventions, international treaties that govern the treatment of prisoners of war.

Whether the benefits of these various anti-terrorism and homeland security initiatives outweigh their costs has been the subject of much passionate debate over the years since 9/11. This debate has only intensified as security costs have mounted. The contributors to *Homeland Security: Current Controversies* reflect the differences of opinion about these critical national security issues.

CHAPTER 1

Is the American Homeland Secure?

Chapter Preface

Since the terrorist attack of September 11, 2001, the U.S. government has waged a highly publicized "war on terror" characterized by large-scale military actions, intensified anti-terror screenings at airports and other public sites, and numerous speeches by public officials warning about the dangers of international terrorism. Some commentators, however, criticize the nation's military-based anti-terror strategy as misdirected. These critics downplay the significance of terrorism, claiming that it is largely a psychological rather than a military threat. In fact, experts say terrorism does not pose a serious physical risk to most Americans; a person is much more likely to be killed in an automobile accident than by terrorists within the United States.

Indeed, most terrorism experts agree that terrorists seek to frighten and disrupt social order as a substitute for their lack of military strength. Interviews with terrorists and studies of terrorist groups suggest that individual terrorists and the groups they represent are often motivated by revenge or a desire to right what they perceive as injustice. Terrorists employ violence as part of a carefully planned and executed strategy designed to further their cause. However, terrorist groups are typically non-government organizations formed by a small number of zealots who have no access to conventional military resources or manpower. To influence governments or those in power, therefore, terrorists resort to nonconventional, asymmetric warfare tactics, such as assassination, kidnapping, hostage-taking, and suicide bombings. Terrorist attacks are also relatively inexpensive and easy to execute by small terrorist organizations with little money to spend or logistical resources at their disposal. In fact, many commentators regard suicide terrorism as the ultimate strategic weapon of the poor and the weak because it inflicts high casualties at a very low cost. Experts thus see terrorism simply as a tactic—violence used by otherwise weak extremist groups.

Terrorism works by attracting media publicity. Suicide bombings or other types of violent and indiscriminate attacks provide an easy story for television reporters, and the attendant media coverage then helps to spread the psychological impact to a wide audience. In fact, the more spectacular the attack, the greater the media attention and fear it garners. This effect can clearly be seen in the 9/11 attack, which had great shock value because of the numbers of people killed and the symbolism of the targets: the World Trade Center, the center of Western finances and economics, and the Pentagon, the heart of the U.S. military establishment. Modern terrorist groups, such as al Qaeda, also like to target civilians, not only because they are easy targets but because the deaths of civilians typically generate the most public outrage and publicity.

Many terrorism experts say that the real purpose of terrorism is to achieve specific political, religious, or ideological goals. By grabbing the public's attention and instilling widespread fear and disorder, terrorists hope to raise awareness of their cause, create pressure to capitulate to their demands, and force political or other concessions from governments or groups that hold power. As terrorism expert Stephen Sloan explains in his 2006 book, *Terrorism: The Present Threat in Context*, "Terrorism is purposeful violence. . . a means to an end and a way to achieve various goals."

A number of terrorism scholars have concluded that most terrorists seek some type of political change, such as the overthrow of a government, a redistribution of wealth, changes in national boundaries, vindication of minority rights, or the establishment of religious governments. University of Chicago political scientist Robert Pape, for example, states in his 2005 book, *Dying to Win: The Strategic Logic of Suicide Terrorism*, that almost all modern suicide terrorist attacks share one common goal: "to compel modern democracies to withdraw military forces from territory that the terrorists consider to be their homeland." Al Qaeda, Pape believes, fits this profile because it seeks changes in U.S. foreign policy, such as the withdrawal of troops from Muslim lands and a reduced U.S. presence in the Middle East.

Other experts, however, point to the recent rise of Islamic fundamentalist terrorist groups (including al Qaeda) and say that religion is the underlying motive for most modern terrorist attacks. According to this view, many Muslims hold very conservative religious views and dislike the spread of Western, secular influences into their societies. They want to remedy this situation by reestablishing a fundamentalist version of Islam and creating Islamic governments that will strictly enforce core, conservative Islamic values. Today's religious terrorists seek to accomplish this through violence. According to the experts, these religious and ideologically motivated terrorist groups tend to be even more violent than previous terrorist movements; their deeply held religious beliefs justify more lethal and massive killings.

If terrorism is primarily a psychological tactic, some commentators have suggested that U.S. officials should seek to downplay the terrorist threat, since publicizing it and stoking public fears about terrorism only aids the terrorists' cause. And if the terrorist threat is not as serious as government officials have suggested, it also may not justify the great expense and effort that has been directed towards the issue since 9/11. Other observers see things differently, however, and maintain that terrorism is one of the gravest threats to U.S. national security. The viewpoints in this chapter explore the critical questions of what level of security is enough in today's post-9/11 world, and whether the government's policies have truly made the American homeland more secure.

Since 9/11, the United States Has Made Extraordinary Progress in Securing the Homeland

The White House

Whitehouse.gov, from which the following viewpoint is taken, is the official Web site of the president of the United States and the president's administration.

[O]n October 9, 2007], the President issued an updated *National Strategy for Homeland Security*, which will serve to guide, organize, and unify our Nation's homeland security efforts. This *Strategy* is a national strategy—not a Federal strategy—and articulates our approach to secure the Homeland over the next several years. It builds on the first *National Strategy for Homeland Security*, issued in July 2002, and complements both the *National Security Strategy* issued in March 2006 and the *National Strategy for Combating Terrorism* issued in September 2006. It reflects our increased understanding of the threats confronting the United States, incorporates lessons learned from exercises and real-world catastrophes, and articulates how we should ensure our long-term success by strengthening the homeland security foundation we have built. This includes calling on Congress to make the Foreign Intelligence Surveillance Act (FISA) reforms in the Protect America Act of 2007 permanent.

Since September 11, 2001, our concept of securing the homeland has evolved, adapting to new realities and threats. The *Strategy* issued today incorporates this increased understanding by:

The White House, "Fact Sheet: National Strategy for Homeland Security," www.white house.gov, October 9, 2007.

- Acknowledging that while we must continue to focus on the persistent and evolving terrorist threat, we also must recognize that certain non-terrorist events that reach catastrophic levels can have significant implications for homeland security.

- Emphasizing that as we secure the Homeland we cannot simply rely on defensive approaches and well-planned response and recovery measures. We recognize that our efforts also must involve offense at home and abroad.

Our National Efforts to Secure the Homeland

The *Strategy* provides a common framework through which our entire Nation—Federal, State, local, and Tribal governments, the private and non-profit sectors, communities, and individual citizens—should focus its homeland security efforts on the following four goals:

1. *Prevent and disrupt terrorist attacks.* To prevent and disrupt terrorist attacks in the United States, we are working to deny terrorists and terrorist-related weapons and materials entry into our country and across all international borders, disrupt terrorists' ability to operate within our borders, and prevent the emergence of violent Islamic radicalization in order to deny terrorists future recruits and to defeat homegrown extremism.

2. *Protect the American people, our critical infrastructure, and key resources.* To protect the lives and livelihoods of the American people, we must undertake measures to deter the threat of terrorism, mitigate the Nation's vulnerability to acts of terror and the full range of man-made and natural catastrophes, and minimize the consequences of an attack or disaster should it occur.

3. *Respond to and recover from incidents that do occur.* To save lives, mitigate suffering, and protect property in future catastrophes, we must strengthen the foundation of an effective, coordinated response. This includes clarifying roles and responsibilities across all levels of government and the private and non-profit sectors. We must also focus on ensuring we have the operational capabilities and flexibility necessary to facilitate both short-term recovery and an effective transition to long-term rebuilding and revitalization efforts.

4. *Continue to strengthen the foundation to ensure our long-term success.* To fulfill these responsibilities over the long term, we will continue to strengthen the principles, systems, structures, and institutions that cut across the homeland security enterprise and support our activities to secure the Homeland. Ultimately, this will help ensure the success of our *Strategy* to secure the Nation. This includes:

• *Applying a comprehensive approach to risk management.* We must apply a risk-based framework across all homeland security efforts in order to identify and assess potential hazards (including their downstream effects), determine what levels of relative risk are acceptable, and prioritize and allocate resources among all homeland security partners, both public and private, to prevent, protect against, and respond to and recover from all manner of incidents.

• *Building a Culture of Preparedness.* Our entire Nation shares common responsibilities in homeland security. In order to help prepare the Nation to carry out these responsibilities, we will continue to foster a Culture of Preparedness that permeates all levels of society—from individual citizens, businesses, and non-profit organizations to Federal, State, local, and Tribal government officials and authorities.

- *Developing a comprehensive Homeland Security Management System.* In order to continue strengthening the foundations of a prepared Nation, we will establish and institutionalize a comprehensive Homeland Security Management System that incorporates all stakeholders. This system involves a continuous, mutually reinforcing cycle of activity across four phases—guidance; planning; execution; and assessment and evaluation. Relevant departments and agencies of the Federal government must take the lead in implementing this system, and State, local, and Tribal governments are highly encouraged to ultimately adopt fully compatible and complementary processes and practices as part of a full-scale national effort. In order to ensure the success of this system, our Nation must further develop a community of homeland security professionals by establishing multidisciplinary education opportunities. In addition to covering homeland and relevant national security issues, this education should include an understanding and appreciation of appropriate regions, religions, cultures, legal systems, and languages. We also must continue to develop interagency and intergovernmental assignments and fellowship opportunities, tying them to promotions and professional advancement.

- *Improving incident management.* We must develop a comprehensive approach to incident management that will help Federal, State, local, and Tribal authorities manage incidents across our goals of prevention, protection, and response and recovery. Our approach will build upon the existing National Incident Management System (NIMS) and help decision-making during crisis and periods of heightened concern.

- *Better utilizing science and technology.* The United States derives much of its strength from its advantage in science and technology, and we must continue to use this advantage and encourage innovative research and development to assist in protecting and defending against the range of natural and man-made threats confronting the Homeland.

- *Using all instruments of national power and influence.* The United States is using its instruments of national power and influence—diplomatic, information, military, economic, financial, intelligence, and law enforcement—to prevent terrorism, protect the lives and livelihoods of the American people, and respond to and recover from incidents. We must build on these efforts, by continuing to enhance our processes for sharing all relevant and appropriate information throughout all levels of government and with our partners, and by prioritizing the continued transformation of our law enforcement and military.

We have greatly increased worldwide counterterrorism efforts since 9/11 ... [making] the United States ... a harder target to strike.

Working with Congress to Make FISA Reforms Permanent, and Other Legislative Action

The U.S. Congress should take bold steps to fulfill its responsibilities in the national effort to secure the Homeland and protect the American people.

- *Congress should help ensure that we have the necessary tools to address changing technologies and homeland security threats while protecting privacy and civil liberties.* We must make additional reforms to the Foreign Intelligence Surveillance Act and ensure that the statute is permanently amended so that our intelligence professionals continue to have the legal tools they need to gather information about the intentions of our enemies while protecting the civil liberties of Americans.

- *Both houses of the Congress should take action to further streamline the organization and structure of those committees that authorize and appropriate homeland security–related funds and otherwise oversee homeland security missions.*

- *The Congress should fully embrace a risk-based funding approach so that we best prioritize our limited resources to meet the most critical homeland security goals and objectives first.*

Progress Made Securing the Homeland

Since September 11, we have made extraordinary progress in securing our Homeland and fighting the War on Terror. We have:

- *Disrupted multiple potentially deadly plots against the United States.* We have greatly increased worldwide counterterrorism efforts since 9/11, which has constrained the ability of al-Qaeda to attack the Homeland and led terrorist groups to find that the United States is a harder target to strike.

- *Strengthened our ability to protect the American people by creating the Department of Homeland Security.* We have also enhanced our homeland security and counterterrorism architecture through the creation of the Office of the Director of National Intelligence, the Homeland Security Council, the National Counterterrorism Center, and U.S. Northern Command, a Department of Defense combatant command focused on homeland defense and civil support.

- *Made our borders more secure.* We are implementing an effective system of layered defense by strengthening the screening of people and goods overseas and by tracking and disrupting the international travel of terrorists.

- *Instituted an active, multi-layered approach that integrates the capabilities of Tribal, local, State and Federal governments, as well as those of the private and non-profit sectors.* In addition, Federal grant funding and technical assistance has also enhanced State, local and Tribal homeland security training and equipment, emergency management capabilities, and the interoperability of communications.

- *Worked with Congress to create, implement, and renew key legal reforms.* The USA PATRIOT Act, the Intelligence Reform and Terrorism Prevention Act of 2004, and the Protect America Act of 2007 promote security and help to implement 9/11 Commission and WMD [weapons of mass destruction] Commission recommendations, while protecting our fundamental liberties.

The U.S. Military Is Better Prepared to Defend Against Terrorist Threats

Jim Garamone

Jim Garamone is a reporter for the American Forces Press Service, a news bureau provided by the American Forces Information Service, part of the United States Department of Defense.

The U.S. military is prepared to defend the United States and support civil authorities in ways not even thought of a decade ago, the assistant secretary of defense for homeland defense said to reporters at the Foreign Press Center here today [December 6, 2007]. Paul McHale said that establishing the office he now holds in the aftermath of the Sept. 11, 2001, terrorist attacks was a recognition that the nature of warfare had changed. "What we recognized was that through most of the history of the United States, in order to fundamentally threaten the national security of our country it required the resources and capabilities of a hostile nation-state," McHale said. "On September 11th it became brutally clear that in the 21st century, with the evolution of destructive technology, the proliferation of that technology and its raw power and transportability, it no longer required the resources of a nation-state to fundamentally threaten the United States."

Confronting the New Terrorist Threat

Small terrorist groups—or even individuals—could gain these technologies and could threaten America. The threat became different and the U.S. response also had to be different. "In order to confront a threat that was more decentralized and less dependent on the command and control of a hostile

Jim Garamone, "Department Works to Keep Homeland Secure," *American Forces Press Service*, December 6, 2007. www.globalsecurity.org.

nation-state ... in order to protect the United States we had to devise defenses that were built upon, but quite different from, defenses that had worked in the Cold War," McHale said.

In 2002, the Defense Department established U.S. Northern Command to coordinate the military defense of the country, and McHale's position was created to supervise all the homeland defense activities of DoD [the Department of Defense]. "The protection of the United States in the 21st century involves much more than military power," McHale said. His office works to coordinate with another newly created entity: the Department of Homeland Security. McHale's office helps ensure defense of the United States, and it provides military assistance to civilian agencies in the event of a catastrophic attack or natural disaster.

The various commands and departments [established by the U.S. Department of Defense since 9/11] have made America safer.

Modifying U.S. Defenses

McHale said the various commands and departments have made America safer. He said U.S. air defense capabilities have been drastically modified since the Sept. 11, 2001, attacks. There are now ground-based air defenses around cities and high-value targets, he said. The air-to-air fighters are "on alert, ready to destroy any aviation threat to the United States," he said. On land, there are active duty and National Guard quick reaction forces ready to deploy in order to defeat a foreign terrorist attack, he said. In the maritime domain, there are Navy and Coast Guard ships ready to interdict and defeat a threat. This could involve "the maritime movement of a weapon of mass destruction—a nuclear device or a dirty bomb," he said.

"We are prepared to use U.S. Navy ships . . . to interdict the maritime approaches to the U.S. We are prepared and train to that mission everyday."

But if the defense fails and a terrorist manages to attack the United States, the office has a mission of providing civil support. The Defense Department could provide manpower, expertise and help to civilian agencies coping with the aftermath of such an attack, McHale said. Communications, equipment, trained manpower, imagery, air assets, there are any number of military capabilities that could help. And it is not limited to an attack. In the aftermath of Hurricane Katrina, the U.S. military helped bring order to an overwhelming humanitarian disaster.

Overall, the nation is in much better shape to defend itself than before September 11, 2001, McHale said. "In terms of physical defense of the United States and our ability to respond, we have many more military personnel with much better equipment, on much shorter alert, task-organized and ready to respond in a way that we did not envision a half-decade ago," McHale said.

The Terrorist Threat Has Been Greatly Exaggerated

John Mueller

John Mueller is an author and a political science professor at Ohio State University.

For the past five years, Americans have been regularly re-galed with dire predictions of another major al Qaeda at-tack in the United States. In 2003, a group of 200 senior gov-ernment officials and business executives, many of them specialists in security and terrorism, pronounced it likely that a terrorist strike more devastating than 9/11—possibly involv-ing weapons of mass destruction—would occur before the end of 2004. In May 2004, Attorney General John Ashcroft warned that al Qaeda could "hit hard" in the next few months and said that 90 percent of the arrangements for an attack on U.S. soil were complete. That fall, *Newsweek* reported that it was "practically an article of faith among counterterrorism of-ficials" that al Qaeda would strike in the run-up to the No-vember 2004 election. When that "October surprise" failed to materialize, the focus shifted: a taped encyclical [message] from Osama bin Laden, it was said, demonstrated that he was too weak to attack before the election but was marshalling his resources to do so months after it. On the first page of its founding manifesto, the massively funded Department of Homeland Security intones, "Today's terrorists can strike at any place, at any time, and with virtually any weapon."

But if it is so easy to pull off an attack and if terrorists are so demonically competent, why have they not done it? Why have they not been sniping at people in shopping centers, col-lapsing tunnels, poisoning the food supply, cutting electrical

John Mueller, "Is There Still a Terrorist Threat?: The Myth of the Omnipresent Enemy," *Foreign Affairs*, September/October 2006. Copyright © 2006 by the Council on Foreign Relations, Inc. Reprinted by permission of Foreign Affairs, www.foreignaffairs.org.

lines, derailing trains, blowing up oil pipelines, causing massive traffic jams, or exploiting the countless other vulnerabilities that, according to security experts, could so easily be exploited? One reasonable explanation is that almost no terrorists exist in the United States and few have the means or the inclination to strike from abroad. But this explanation is rarely offered.

Huffing and Puffing

Instead, Americans are told—often by the same people who had once predicted imminent attacks—that the absence of international terrorist strikes in the United States is owed to the protective measures so hastily and expensively put in place after 9/11. But there is a problem with this argument. True, there have been no terrorist incidents in the United States in the last five years. But nor were there any in the five years before the 9/11 attacks, at a time when the United States was doing much less to protect itself. It would take only one or two guys with a gun or an explosive to terrorize vast numbers of people, as the sniper attacks around Washington, D.C., demonstrated in 2002. Accordingly, the government's protective measures would have to be nearly perfect to thwart all such plans. Given the monumental imperfection of the government's response to Hurricane Katrina, and the debacle of FBI [Federal Bureau of Investigation] and National Security Agency programs to upgrade their computers to better coordinate intelligence information, that explanation seems farfetched. Moreover, Israel still experiences terrorism even with a far more extensive security apparatus.

It may well have become more difficult for terrorists to get into the country, but, as thousands demonstrate each day, it is far from impossible. Immigration procedures have been substantially tightened (at considerable cost), and suspicious U.S. border guards have turned away a few likely bad apples. But visitors and immigrants continue to flood the country. There are over 300 million legal entries by foreigners each year, and illegal crossings number between 1,000 and 4,000 a day—to say nothing of the generous quantities of forbidden substances that the government has been unable to intercept or even detect despite decades of a strenuous and well-funded "war on drugs." Every year, a number of people from Muslim countries—perhaps hundreds—are apprehended among the illegal flow from Mexico, and many more probably make it through. Terrorism does not require a large force. And the 9/11 planners, assuming Middle Eastern males would have problems entering the United States legally after the attack, put into motion plans to rely thereafter on non-Arabs with passports from Europe and Southeast Asia.

If al Qaeda operatives are as determined and inventive as assumed, they should be here by now.

If al Qaeda operatives are as determined and inventive as assumed, they should be here by now. If they are not yet here, they must not be trying very hard or must be far less dedicated, diabolical, and competent than the common image would suggest.

Another popular explanation for the fact that there have been no more attacks asserts that the invasion of Afghanistan in 2001, although it never managed to snag bin Laden, severely disrupted al Qaeda and its operations. But this claim is similarly unconvincing. The 2004 train bombings in Madrid [Spain] were carried out by a tiny group of men who had never been to Afghanistan, much less to any of al Qaeda's training camps. They pulled off a coordinated nonsuicidal attack with 13 remote-controlled bombs, ten of which went off on schedule, killing 191 and injuring more than 1,800. The experience with that attack, as well as with the London [United Kingdom] bombings of 2005, suggests that, as the former U.S. counterterrorism officials Daniel Benjamin and Steven Simon have noted, for a terrorist attack to succeed, "all that is necessary are the most portable, least detectable tools of the terrorist trade: ideas."

It is also sometimes suggested that the terrorists are now too busy killing Americans and others in Iraq to devote the time, manpower, or energy necessary to pull off similar deeds in the United States. But terrorists with al Qaeda sympathies or sensibilities have managed to carry out attacks in Egypt, Jordan, Morocco, Saudi Arabia, Spain, Turkey, the United Kingdom, and elsewhere in the past three years; not every single potential bomb thrower has joined the fray in Iraq.

Perhaps, some argue, terrorists are unable to mount attacks in the United States because the Muslim community there, unlike in many countries in Europe, has been well integrated into society. But the same could be said about the United Kingdom, which experienced a significant terrorist attack in 2005. And European countries with less well-integrated Muslim communities, such as Germany, France, and Norway, have yet to experience al Qaeda terrorism. Indeed, if terrorists are smart, they will avoid Muslim communities because that is the lamppost under which policing agencies are most intensely searching for them. The perpetrators of the 9/11 attacks were ordered generally to stay away from mosques and American Muslims. That and the Madrid plot show that tiny terrorist conspiracies hardly need a wider support network to carry out their schemes.

Another common explanation is that al Qaeda is craftily biding its time. But what for? The 9/11 attacks took only about two years to prepare. The carefully coordinated, very destructive, and politically productive terrorist attacks in Madrid in 2004 were conceived, planned from scratch, and then executed all within six months; the bombs were set off less than two months after the conspirators purchased their first supplies of dynamite, paid for with hashish. . . . Given the extreme provocation of the invasion of Iraq in 2003, one would think that terrorists might be inclined to shift their timetable into higher gear. And if they are so patient, why do they continually claim that another attack is just around the corner? It was in 2003 that al Qaeda's top leaders promised attacks in Australia, Bahrain, Egypt, Italy, Japan, Jordan, . . . Kuwait, Qatar, Saudi Arabia, the United States, and Yemen. Three years later, some bombs had gone off in Saudi Arabia, Egypt, Yemen, and Jordan but not in any other of the explicitly threatened countries. Those attacks were tragic, but their sparseness could be taken as evidence that it is not only American alarmists who are given to extravagant huffing and puffing.

The threat posed by homegrown or imported terrorists . . . has been massively exaggerated.

Terrorists Under the Bed

A fully credible explanation for the fact that the United States has suffered no terrorist attacks since 9/11 is that the threat posed by homegrown or imported terrorists—like that presented by Japanese Americans during World War II or by American Communists after it—has been massively exaggerated. Is it possible that the haystack is essentially free of needles?

The FBI embraces a spooky I-think-therefore-they-are line of reasoning when assessing the purported terrorist menace. In 2003, its director, Robert Mueller, proclaimed, "The greatest threat is from al Qaeda cells in the U.S. that we have not yet identified." He rather mysteriously deemed the threat from those unidentified entities to be "increasing in part because of the heightened publicity" surrounding such episodes as the 2002 Washington sniper shootings and the 2001 anthrax attacks (which had nothing to do with al Qaeda). But in 2001, the 9/11 hijackers received no aid from U.S.-based al Qaeda operatives for the simple reason that no such operatives appear to have existed. It is not at all clear that that condition has changed.

Mueller also claimed to know that "al Qaeda maintains the ability and the intent to inflict significant casualties in the U.S. with little warning." If this was true—if the terrorists had both the ability and the intent in 2003, and if the threat they presented was somehow increasing—they had remained remarkably quiet by the time the unflappable Mueller repeated his alarmist mantra in 2005: "I remain very concerned about what we are not seeing."

Intelligence estimates in 2002 held that there were as many as 5,000 al Qaeda terrorists and supporters in the United States. However, a secret FBI report in 2005 wistfully noted that although the bureau had managed to arrest a few bad guys here and there after more than three years of intense and well-funded hunting, it had been unable to identify a single true al Qaeda sleeper cell anywhere in the country. Thousands of people in the United States have had their overseas communications monitored under a controversial warrantless surveillance program. Of these, fewer than ten U.S. citizens or residents per year have aroused enough suspicion to impel the agencies spying on them to seek warrants authorizing surveillance of their domestic communications as well; none of this activity, it appears, has led to an indictment on any charge whatever.

Only a small number of people picked up on terrorism charges . . . have been convicted.

In addition to massive eavesdropping and detention programs, every year some 30,000 "national security letters" are issued without judicial review, forcing businesses and other institutions to disclose confidential information about their customers without telling anyone they have done so. That process has generated thousands of leads that, when pursued, have led nowhere. Some 80,000 Arab and Muslim immigrants have been subjected to fingerprinting and registration, another 8,000 have been called in for interviews with the FBI, and over 5,000 foreign nationals have been imprisoned in initiatives designed to prevent terrorism. This activity, notes the Georgetown University law professor David Cole, has not resulted in a single conviction for a terrorist crime. In fact, only a small number of people picked up on terrorism charges—always to great official fanfare—have been convicted at all, and almost all of these convictions have been for other infractions, particularly immigration violations. Some of those convicted have clearly been mental cases or simply flaunting jihadist bravado—rattling on about taking down the Brooklyn Bridge with a blowtorch, blowing up the Sears Tower if only they could get to Chicago, beheading the prime minister of Canada, or flooding lower Manhattan by somehow doing something terrible to one of those tunnels.

Appetite for Destruction?

One reason al Qaeda and "al Qaeda types" seem not to be trying very hard to repeat 9/11 may be that that dramatic act of destruction itself proved counterproductive by massively heightening concerns about terrorism around the world. No matter how much they might disagree on other issues (most notably on the war in Iraq), there is a compelling incentive for states—even ones such as Iran, Libya, Sudan, and Syria—to cooperate in cracking down on al Qaeda, because they know that they could easily be among its victims. The FBI may not have uncovered much of anything within the United States since 9/11, but thousands of apparent terrorists have been rounded, or rolled, up overseas with U.S. aid and encouragement.

Although some Arabs and Muslims took pleasure in the suffering inflicted on 9/11 . . . the most common response among jihadists and religious nationalists was a vehement rejection of al Qaeda's strategy and methods. When Soviet troops invaded Afghanistan in 1979, there were calls for jihad everywhere in Arab and Muslim lands, and tens of thousands flocked to the country to fight the invaders. In stark contrast, when the U.S. military invaded in 2001 to topple an Islamist regime, there was, as the political scientist Fawaz Gerges points out, a "deafening silence" from the Muslim world, and only a trickle of jihadists went to fight the Americans. Other jihadists publicly blamed al Qaeda for their post-9/11 problems and held the attacks to be shortsighted and hugely miscalculated.

The post-9/11 willingness of governments around the world to take on international terrorists has been much reinforced and amplified by subsequent, if scattered, terrorist activity outside the United States. Thus, a terrorist bombing in Bali in 2002 galvanized the Indonesian government into action. Extensive arrests and convictions—including of leaders who had previously enjoyed some degree of local fame and political popularity—seem to have severely degraded the capacity of the chief jihadist group in Indonesia, Jemaah Islamiyah. After terrorists attacked Saudis in Saudi Arabia in 2003, that country, very much for self-interested reasons, became considerably more serious about dealing with domestic terrorism; it soon clamped down on radical clerics and preachers. Some rather inept terrorist bombings in Casablanca in 2003 inspired a similarly determined crackdown by Moroccan authorities. And the 2005 bombing in Jordan of a wedding at a hotel (an unbelievably stupid target for the terrorists) succeeded mainly in outraging the Jordanians: according to a Pew poll, the percentage of the population expressing a lot of confidence in bin Laden to "do the right thing" dropped from 25 percent to less than one percent after the attack.

Threat Perceptions

The results of policing activity overseas suggest that the absence of results in the United States has less to do with terrorists' cleverness or with investigative incompetence than with the possibility that few, if any, terrorists exist in the country. It also suggests that al Qaeda's ubiquity and capacity to do damage may have, as with so many perceived threats, been exaggerated. Just because some terrorists may wish to do great harm does not mean that they are able to.

Gerges argues that mainstream Islamists—who make up the vast majority of the Islamist political movement—gave up on the use of force before 9/11, except perhaps against Israel, and that the jihadists still committed to violence constitute a tiny minority. Even this small group primarily focuses on various "infidel" Muslim regimes and considers jihadists who carry out violence against the "far enemy"—mainly Europe and the United States—to be irresponsible, reckless adventurers who endanger the survival of the whole movement. In this view, 9/11 was a sign of al Qaeda's desperation, isolation, fragmentation, and decline, not of its strength.

The lifetime chance of an American being killed by international terrorism is about one in 80,000—about the same chance of being killed by a comet or a meteor.

Those attacks demonstrated, of course, that al Qaeda—or at least 19 of its members—still possessed some fight. And none of this is to deny that more terrorist attacks on the United States are still possible. Nor is it to suggest that al Qaeda is anything other than a murderous movement. Moreover, after the ill-considered U.S. venture in Iraq is over, freelance jihadists trained there may seek to continue their operations elsewhere—although they are more likely to focus on places such as Chechnya [part of Russia] than on the United States. A unilateral American military attack against Iran could cause that country to retaliate, probably with very wide support within the Muslim world, by aiding anti-

American insurgencies in Afghanistan and Iraq and inflicting damage on Israel and on American interests worldwide.

But while keeping such potential dangers in mind, it is worth remembering that the total number of people killed since 9/11 by al Qaeda or al Qaeda–like operatives outside of Afghanistan and Iraq is not much higher than the number who drown in bathtubs in the United States in a single year, and that the lifetime chance of an American being killed by international terrorism is about one in 80,000—about the same chance of being killed by a comet or a meteor. Even if there were a 9/11-scale attack every three months for the next five years, the likelihood that an individual American would number among the dead would be two hundredths of a percent (or one in 5,000).

Although it remains heretical to say so, the evidence so far suggests that fears of the omnipotent terrorist—reminiscent of those inspired by images of the 20-foot-tall Japanese after Pearl Harbor or the 20-foot-tall Communists at various points in the Cold War [the ideological struggle between the United States and the former Soviet Union]—may have been overblown, the threat presented within the United States by al Qaeda greatly exaggerated. The massive and expensive homeland security apparatus erected since 9/11 may be persecuting some, spying on many, inconveniencing most, and taxing all to defend the United States against an enemy that scarcely exists.

Homeland Security Efforts Since 9/11 Have Been Ineffective and Wasteful

Stephen Cass

Stephen Cass is a senior editor at Discover, *a science and technology magazine.*

Six years after the fall of the Twin Towers [World Trade Center in New York City], the devastating blow to the Pentagon, and the inspiring courage of the passengers and crew of United Airlines Flight 93, antiterrorism funding is an exercise in pork-barrel spending and high-profile projects of dubious value.

In our effort to thwart terrorists, we're making things easier for them.

On the one hand, we have money being spent on petty projects designed to defend "targets" that are more at risk from a meteor strike than a terrorist attack, like the town of Madisonville, Texas. As reported by *The Dallas Morning News*, the town, population 4,200, used a federal homeland security grant to purchase a $30,000 customized trailer. The trailer can be used as a mobile command center, but city officials admitted it is more likely to be used as an information and first-aid booth during the town's annual mushroom festival. Or there's the story of Dillingham, Alaska, population 2,400. Last year, the *Anchorage Daily News* noted that Dillingham—which doesn't have a single street light—had received $202,000 dollars in homeland security funding to purchase surveillance cameras. On the other hand, the danger of big, headline-grabbing threats has been ameliorated to a limited extent—but these threats, like dirty bombs or bioterrorism, have always been inherently unlikely to come to pass on anything like the apocalyptic scale feared by some.

Ironically, in our effort to thwart terrorists, we're making things easier for them. Without lifting a finger and starting down the long, difficult, and expensive road of actually making a viable biological, chemical, or nuclear weapon of mass destruction, the terrorists have managed to distract us with the specter of such a device. Meanwhile, we remain vulnerable to other, less dramatic but perhaps much more realistic lines of attack.

The Non-Threat of Dirty Bombs

Let's start with dirty bombs, a staple of media-fed fears. In the typical scenario, a group of terrorists steal a few ounces of radioactive material like cobalt 60 from a food irradiation facility. This cannot be used to make a nuclear bomb, but it gives a lethal radiation dose in close quarters. The terrorists wrap the cobalt 60 around a conventional explosive, detonate it, and shower a city with deadly fallout. To detect dirty bombs in the offing, gamma and other radiation detectors have been deployed to airports and seaports as well as police departments around the country. But there are still many unprotected ports. If drug cartels can regularly sneak tons of narcotics into and around the country, surely terrorists can do the same with a much smaller cache of radioactive material.

What is really keeping us safe is probably not those radiation detectors but the basic physics of trying to carry out a radioactive attack. In order to contaminate a large area with enough radioactive material to pose a major health hazard, the dirty bomb would have to be packed with so much cobalt

60 (on the order of a few ounces in this case) that the terrorists would die of radiation poisoning within minutes of exposure to their own weapon.

A practical dirty bomb's main effects would be from fear, not radiation, with both the Department of Homeland Security and the American Institute of Physics predicting few deaths from cancer or radiation poisoning, even in densely populated areas. "The radioactivity released by dirty bombs is not life threatening," says Angelo Acquista, former medical director of the Office of Emergency Management in New York City and author of *The Survival Guide: What to Do in a Biological, Chemical, or Nuclear Emergency*. Writing in MIT's *Technology Review*, Richard Muller, a senior scientist at the Lawrence Berkeley National Laboratory in California, calculated the radiation exposure—measured in a unit known as the rem—that city residents would receive from a practical dirty bomb. His analysis concluded that no one would receive sufficient radiation to induce radiation illness, let alone death, and that the longterm risk of developing cancer was only fractionally increased.

But with lawmakers and government agencies ratcheting up the rhetoric about dirty bombs in their lobbying for more funding, the average citizen can hardly be blamed for considering dirty bombs a grave threat—a perfect example of well-intentioned efforts that would amplify, not dampen, the impact of a terrorist attack.

As with dirty bombs, the main thing keeping us safe from bio-attack is the nature of the weapon itself.

The Hype About Bioterrorism

Bioterrorism is another overhyped threat. According to the Center for Arms Control and Non-Proliferation, based in Washington, D.C., since 2001 federal and state governments have spent $41.5 billion combating bioterrorism, with another $6.8 billion on the way. The money has been spent on things like improving sensors to detect an attack and on building up a stockpile of drugs to combat various pathogens like anthrax. Faced with the prospect of terrorists releasing a bioweapon that spawns a deadly nationwide epidemic, quickly overwhelming hospitals and other health services, surely this seems a reasonable outlay. As with dirty bombs, the main thing keeping us safe from bio-attack is the nature of the weapon itself. The most dangerous and virulent pathogens, like the Ebola virus, kill their victims too quickly, so an infected person is able to spread the disease to only a relatively small number of people before succumbing. According to the Centers for Disease Control and Prevention, Ebola has an incubation period of 2 to 21 days and kills 50 to 90 percent of those infected within two weeks of the onset of symptoms. This produces terrifying but limited and short-lived outbreaks. The second problem terrorists face is how to infect victims with their disease of choice. Aerosolizing the pathogen—so that it can be released and inhaled by a large number of people—is an obvious approach, but this is difficult to do, not least because many infectious agents can't survive long outside a host.

Anthrax is seen as a particular threat because it occurs in spore form, meaning that it can be transported easily and will remain potent for decades. In principle, inhaling just a couple of spores could spark a fatal infection. More realistically, being exposed to several thousand spores would be required for most people to develop symptoms, but that still amounts to a dose weighing far less than a millionth of an ounce.

It's no surprise, then, that anthrax was used in the still-unsolved bioterror mailings that occurred in the weeks after 9/11. The attacks sparked frenzied countermeasures among the general public, with people ironing their mail to kill spores and reports of people attempting to obtain personal stockpiles of the antibiotic Cipro. The government set up more elaborate schemes to use electron beams to sterilize mail. Yet despite the mailings' status as the most sophisticated and deadly series of bioterrorist attacks in the United States to date, just five people were killed and another 17 sickened. Compare this with the average annual death toll of 36,000 Americans from ordinary influenza.

Chemical weapons are a more clearly evident risk.

The Real Threat of Chemical Weapons

Chemical weapons are a more clearly evident risk: The sarin nerve gas that cultists used to attack the Tokyo subway killed 12 and injured hundreds in 1995. As a consequence, stockpiles of the nerve gas antidote, called Chempacks, have been put in place in cities around America, and detection systems are being developed to warn of an attack and have already been deployed in a few places like Grand Central Terminal in New York City. First responders have also been provided with field supplies of nerve gas antidote, with each ambulance in New York City, for example, carrying 60 Mark I kits, says Neal Richmond, former deputy medical director of the New York Fire Department. Each Mark I kit has two autoinjectors, one containing atropine, which works to counteract the immediate effects of the nerve gas, and the other a drug called 2-PAM, which helps the body clear the nerve gas out of its system.

All that said, for those caught in a chemical attack, the available countermeasures are not exactly reassuring. A chemical weapons attack would be a "mass casualty event," Richmond warns, meaning that emergency responders would expect to be overwhelmed by the number of sick and dying people. In such an event, the rules for treating victims that most people have come to expect from emergency responders are altered. "You want to use available resources to get the greatest benefit for the greatest number of people instead of focusing all your resources on the sickest people," Richmond says. Rather than treating the sickest first, rescuers would treat the most likely to survive first, evacuating those who can walk or crawl to a decontamination area before sorting out the rest.

In a chemical attack, the task of first responders would be further complicated by their bulky protective suits. These make normal medical examinations impossible, forcing responders to rely on "noxious stimulus triage"—nicknamed kick triage—to sort out the living from the dead. "You don't really kick them, but you do shake them, move them" to see if they react, says Richmond. "Anyone who doesn't appear dead gets dragged out" and injected with three Mark I kits. If that stabilizes the victim long enough to reach hospital care, chances are he will survive, as more antidote can be administered as needed to keep counteracting the nerve gas. If the victim's condition worsens before he can reach the hospital, however, he is unlikely to receive any additional antidote— especially if the antidote is in short supply—as the responders turn their attention to others. Richmond worries that despite all the elaborate planning made by the Department of Homeland Security and others to deal with chemical and biological attacks, mundane but important things aren't happening—like conducting enough drills to make sure that these plans actually get implemented properly. He also notes that a lot of money has been spent preparing for rare attacks, but emergency rooms around the country already have difficulties coping with routine patients: "We need to tackle building the everyday infrastructure in this country so that it's working for every patient, every day. Then when the big things come down, we'll be pretty prepared."

An Issue of Funding

Another big part of the homeland security boondoggle is the formula used to dole out federal funds. Originally, after 9/11, homeland security funds were distributed according to a formula that first guaranteed each and every state a certain minimum level of funding and then divvied up remaining funds according to the size of state populations. Not surprisingly, the 9/11 Commission was horrified by such a simplistic approach, which gave money to states whether it was needed or not. Consequently, the commission recommended in its 2004 report that funding be based "solely on risks and vulnerabilities, putting New York City and Washington, D.C., at the top of the current list."

Since then, there have been attempts to reform the formula to distribute funds based on the actual risk posed by terrorists. Unfortunately, these attempts have resulted in sometimes ridiculous results. Last year's much-derided analysis by the Department of Homeland Security reduced New York City's homeland security funding by 40 percent to $124 million, concluding that the metropolis contained no national monuments or icons—somehow skipping over the Statue of Liberty, the Empire State Building, the Brooklyn Bridge, and Wall Street, among others. Although some of New York's funding was eventually restored, the homeland security distribution formula is still far off the mark set by the 9/11 Commission.

And so pork still abounds, prompting Congressmen Anthony Weiner and Jeff Flake to produce a list last March of the most absurd homeland security grants they could find. Standouts included $36,000 to Kentucky in 2005 to prevent terrorists from raising money at state bingo halls; $7,348 worth of bulletproof vests for the police and fire department dogs of Columbus, Ohio, in the same year; and the biggest whopper of them all, $8,000 in 2006 for a Wisconsin fire department's clown and puppet shows.

The only silver lining is that these absurd preparations are probably not going to be needed. Why? Because terrorists like getting as much bang for their buck as anyone else, which is why conventional explosives, not exotic weapons of mass destruction, will probably continue to be their primary weapon of choice. "The reality is that conventional weapons are easier to manufacture, transport, and detonate," says Acquista, a point graphically illustrated by the recent propane-based car-bomb attacks in the United Kingdom.

The Best Advice: Stay Home

But let's imagine a worst-case scenario: A particularly advanced terrorist group does manage to set off a dirty bomb, or a bioweapon begins to spread throughout the population. The natural instinct—evacuate—may not be your best option, and in fact most Department of Homeland Security plans do not envision anything like attempting to evacuate an entire city except in the extremely unlikely event of the aftermath of an atomic bomb blast.

Mostly this is because these kinds of attacks are much more limited in their geographic impact than our fear would lead us to believe and also because evacuating cities quickly is very difficult, as was demonstrated by New Orleans and the Hurricane Katrina debacle. Even on 9/11, when the destruction was confined to a small area of Lower Manhattan, it took six to seven hours to evacuate around 400,000 commuters by boat. With the subways out of commission, another 2.5 million Manhattan commuters made their way home as best they could, taking many hours in most cases and clogging bridges and roads.

Should the worst happen, unless your dwelling is in immediate danger, the best advice may be to ignore all the government-fueled drama and stay home, at least temporarily. Following an atomic blast, for example, "after seven days, the radiation goes down about 90 percent," says Acquista, making evacuation at that time much safer. Acquista recommends sheltering underground in such a circumstance, which allows as much radiation as possible to be blocked by the ground and buildings above. In the event of a chemical attack, though, he recommends staying indoors aboveground, because nerve agents are heavier than air and hence will accumulate in basements. And although the suggestion that citizens keep duct tape and plastic sheeting on hand was much reviled when made in 2003 by then Secretary for Homeland Security Tom Ridge, Acquista believes it would be useful in a chemical attack to seal a refuge with tape and sheeting until the danger passes, because "most chemicals dissipate very rapidly." Homeland security, it seems, really does begin at home.

The Government Has Let Homeland Security Languish Since 9/11

James Ridgeway

James Ridgeway is an investigative journalist and Washington, D.C., bureau chief for Mother Jones *magazine, a nonprofit publication devoted to social justice.*

Six years after 9/11 and three years after the 9/11 Commission, Congress has just started to do what's necessary to protect us from the next terror attack. But have they done enough? And is time running out?. . .

The Bush administration has gone to war, detained enemy combatants in Guantanamo, and let executive power run amok, all in the name of combating terrorism. Yet its real approach to protecting us from another 9/11 is best summed up in the words of its 2002 *National Homeland Security Strategy*, which declared that the federal government "should fund only those homeland security activities that are not supplied, or are inadequately supplied, in the market. . . . [M]any homeland security activities, such as intelligence gathering and border security, are properly accomplished at the federal level." In other words, airlines should improve their own screening methods, skyscraper tenants should develop their own evacuation plans, and the rest of us should stock up on duct tape.

Yet actually protecting the homeland demands actions that are ideologically abhorrent to most Republicans, and politically risky for either party, such as expanding federal regulation, increasing federal spending, hiring unionized federal workers, and facing down industries with powerful lobbies— from airlines and oil companies to the chemical industry.

James Ridgeway, "Homeland Insecurity," *Mother Jones*, September 5, 2007. Reproduced by permission. www.motherjones.com.

"Even though the most tempting targets for terrorists are those that can produce widespread economic and social disruption, the White House has declared that safeguarding the nation's critical infrastructure is not a federal responsibility," says Stephen Flynn, a former Coast Guard commander who now studies homeland security at the Council on Foreign Relations. . . .

Congressional Anti-Terror Efforts

Congressional Democrats have made a nominally more serious effort to address some of these threats. The party's leadership made homeland security a key issue in the 2006 [congressional] election, promising to enact all the reforms that had been proposed by the 9/11 Commission [officially called the National Commission on Terrorist Attacks, which was established to provide a detailed account of the circumstances surrounding the September 11, 2001, attacks on America, and to make recommendations designed to guard against future attacks]. Its recommendations, outlined in its July 2004 report, had been low priorities for the Republican Congress and the Bush administration (which had originally opposed the creation of the commission—and after acquiescing to its creation, starved it of funding, time, and information). A "report card" issued by former commission members in December 2005 gave the government D's, F's, or "incompletes" in half of the categories, and little additional progress was made in the following year. Rep. Bennie Thompson, the Mississippi Democrat who took over as chair of the House Homeland Security Committee in January 2007, told *Mother Jones* that Congress faces "a real challenge. The Bush administration talks tough, but when it comes to doing those things that absolutely have to take place for people to be secure, they leave a lot to be desired." In many vital areas, Thompson said, we are "flying by the seat of our pants."

Thompson claims that under his leadership, his committee has become "more aggressive," scheduling hearings with real "subpoena power" and giving its subcommittee chairpersons new latitude to pursue tough investigations. But P.J. Crowley, a homeland security expert at the Center for American Progress [a progressive think tank located in Washington, D.C.], said that the current committee structure in Congress makes a comprehensive approach to domestic security matters difficult. In the past, some 80 different committees and subcommittees have had a hand in homeland security. House majority leader Nancy Pelosi has cut that number down to 55. But the feuding and jockeying for power remains intense—so much so, Crowley says, that drinking water and wastewater, for example, have been exempted from security measures passed by Congress because "committees that do environmental issues didn't want to cede these issues to [those that do] homeland security."

In one of her first moves after the Democrats took charge of Congress last fall, Pelosi pushed a set of reforms known as the Implementing the 9/11 Commission Recommendations Act of 2007 through the House without debate. Shortly thereafter, the Senate passed its own version of the bill, the Improving America's Security Act. However, a compromise version of the measure was predictably delayed by committee haggling, and again by a provision authorizing airport security workers to join unions, which President Bush promised to veto. The provision was dropped and the bill was passed and signed by the president just before Congress recessed for the summer [2007].

Democrats tried to make political hay over the moment. Democratic National Committee chairman Howard Dean crowed, "Today Democrats did what President Bush and Republicans refused to do. . . . It's no wonder that Americans trust Democrats more than Republicans to keep them safe." On the House floor, Pelosi proclaimed, "With this bill, we'll be keeping our promises to the families of 9/11. We'll be honoring the work of the 9/11 Commission; and we'll be making the American people safer."

Well, maybe. The legislation sets a five-year deadline for the screening of all ship containers coming into the United States, but it also allows the secretary of Homeland Security to extend the deadline in two-year increments. The law orders all cargo carried on a passenger aircraft to be screened—not by people but by machines, which to date are imperfect at best. It aims to create a communications system linking federal, state, and local officials in real time. And it calls for homeland security grants to the states to be distributed on the basis of risk—so, in theory, New York would receive more money than, say, North Dakota. But actually funding and implementing the program requires the approval of congressional appropriations committees.

Actually protecting the homeland demands actions that are . . . politically risky.

Resources for First Responders

Relative to what's truly at stake, the new legislation calls for only a fraction of what is needed, both in terms of funding and regulatory muscle. Yet its basic provisions show some appreciation of the fundamental truths underlying homeland security. First, future attacks on the United States in all likelihood will be aimed at basic infrastructure—bridges, tunnels, rail lines, and ports in heavily populated areas. Second, the federal government lacks a plan, much less an actual system, for protecting these targets. Third, there has been only minimal progress at the federal level in setting standards, building communication networks, or providing adequate risk-based funding that would enable local governments and the private sector to improve their security measures. And finally, what happens in the event of an attack—how many live and how many die—depends not on the federal government or the military, but largely on local first responders and emergency management operations.

Six years after 9/11, most first responders still lack the resources and equipment they need to save lives.

Yet six years after 9/11, most first responders still lack the resources and equipment they need to save lives. As Flynn points out, emergency providers are unlikely to have any backup for the first 12 to 24 hours following an attack. (And with so much of the National Guard overseas, they may have little backup even after a day.) Fire departments have enough radios for only half their shifts, and only a third of the needed breathing apparatuses. Emergency medical technicians don't have the equipment to tell what chemical or biological agent was used in an attack. And police officers do not have protective gear they'd need to secure the site of a chemical or biological attack.

Strengthening Security Is a Work in Progress

The Plain Dealer

The Plain Dealer is Cleveland, Ohio's primary newspaper and the state's largest daily news publication.

In the aftermath of the 9/11 attacks, the Bush administration and Congress rushed to shore up national security and reassure Americans of a determination to foil future threats. The mere fact that six years have passed without another major attack on U.S. soil indicates that some of those efforts worked.

Strengthening national security—in ways that are practical and that respect the very values that set America apart from its enemies—remains very much a work in progress.

Patriot Act Ruled Unconstitutional

But [September 2007] brought two reminders that strengthening national security—in ways that are practical and that respect the very values that set America apart from its enemies—remains very much a work in progress. One of Washington's first responses to the attacks was to pass the USA Patriot Act, billed as giving federal investigators new weapons to track and disrupt terrorist activities within this country. One of those weapons expanded the previously limited ability of federal investigators to obtain e-mail and telephone data from telecommunications firms without first obtaining a warrant. The new law also made it illegal for the firms that received these "national security letters" to reveal the request or appeal it.

The Plain Dealer, "Making the Homeland Secure Is Slow Going—An Editorial," September 11, 2007. Reproduced by permission. www.cleveland.com.

After two federal courts struck down those provisions, Congress amended the Patriot Act in 2005. But U.S. District Judge Victor Marrero of New York has now ruled that it is still "the legislative equivalent of breaking and entering, with an ominous free pass to the hijacking of constitutional values." Marrero's 102-page decision reserves special umbrage for a provision in the amended law that allows for judicial review but virtually dictates that outcome by instructing courts to go along with any gag order the FBI [Federal Bureau of Investigation] swears is necessary.

The administration undoubtedly will challenge Marrero's ruling, but in light of the FBI's own admission earlier this year that it has frequently broken its own rules for using national security letters, the judge's words carry all the more weight. As initially conceived and even amended, the Patriot Act sought to short-circuit a process of prior review that has served this country well for more than 200 years. It represented overreaching born of fear.

Six years [after 9/11], the challenge of accomplishing change [in homeland security] that is both intelligent and meaningful remains.

Criticism of the Department of Homeland Security

The very day Marrero issued his ruling, the nonpartisan Government Accountability Office reported that the Department of Homeland Security was failing to meet many of its most basic goals. Mostly notably, government auditors concluded that the department has not done enough to prepare for the aftermath of a major attack or natural disaster—as residents of the region devastated by Hurricane Katrina can testify—or to clear the way for information-sharing across bureaucratic lines.

That's not entirely unexpected. The new department opened for business on March 1, 2003, and brought together 22 agencies with 220,000 employees. Getting them to work harmoniously in just four years isn't very realistic—especially when 86 different congressional committees still claim to oversee the department's many components. But that will be scant comfort if, God forbid, the department has to deal with another tragedy. Focus and urgency are needed.

In the awful days after the Twin Towers [the World Trade Center in New York City] and the Pentagon were attacked, everyone agreed that America had to change. Six years later, the challenge of accomplishing change that is both intelligent and meaningful remains.

Americans Remain Attractive Terrorist Targets

The Economist

The Economist *is a weekly British newspaper that focuses on political and economic news.*

How safe is America now? Americans remain attractive targets. On September 5th [2007] the German authorities said they had foiled a plot to bomb American military facilities [in Germany]. According to the latest National Intelligence Estimate, a rejuvenated al-Qaeda operating in tribal areas of Pakistan is determined to launch a catastrophic attack on American soil using chemical, biological or nuclear weapons. It has become a cliche in Washington to point out that the question is not whether terrorists, al-Qaeda or other, will strike the United States again, but when and how. Yet no foreign terrorist has managed to strike the country since September 11th, 2001. Republican candidates have run on—and won on—that fact, which continues to buoy an otherwise ever more unpopular [President] George Bush. It's an impressive record, but is it the Republicans' to claim?

The Bush administration has taken care of many of the basics since 2001. Cockpit doors have been reinforced, more air marshals patrol the skies, and better records are kept on those entering the country. Co-operation between America and other countries on anti-terror efforts has also increased, which contributed to the arrest in London last year of a band of terrorists plotting to bring down aircraft over the Atlantic. More impressive achievements, some experts say, are in the pipeline.

The most obvious change since the 2001 attacks has been the added rigmarole at American airports. Passengers must

The Economist, "Six Years On; Homeland Security (How Safe Is America?)," vol. 384, September 8, 2007, p. 35. © 2007 Economist Newspaper Ltd. Republished with permission of Economist Newspaper Ltd., conveyed through Copyright Clearance Center, Inc.

now remove their shoes for x-ray. The amount and type of liquid allowed through security checkpoints is strictly regulated. Non-Americans entering the country are photographed and fingerprinted.

Critics have long complained, however, that federal antiterrorism programmes have followed threats, not anticipated them. Footwear did not receive such scrutiny before would-be bomber Richard Reid tried to light the explosives packed into his shoes on a transatlantic flight. The Transportation Security Administration, which governs airport security, did not produce its liquids policy until British investigators disrupted last year's plot to blow up America-bound flights by combining household chemicals.

Stopping more ambitious attacks ... is still probably at least as much a matter of luck as of skill.

The authorities also seem to have trouble implementing policies already in place. Government reports suggest that airline security procedures are remarkably ineffective, routinely failing to catch explosive materials carried by undercover agents. Low morale and high turnover plague the Department of Homeland Security, a 180,000-person behemoth set up after the 2001 attacks. American border officials check who is entering the country, but do not reliably record who leaves (or, more important, who doesn't).

A lot of money has also been wasted in the past six years. Congress, for example, has a programme that guarantees homeland-security grants to each state government regardless of risk. Calculations of risk have been odd in the past, too, as when Washington, DC, was classified as at low-risk of terrorist attack, or when New York City had no national monuments or icons listed on a Department of Homeland Security registry. Indiana boasted the most potential terror targets of any state. The formulas have since been rejigged, but critics say they still send too much money to areas of the country that do not really need it.

American efforts aside, al-Qaeda's desire to cause spectacular damage to internationally prominent monuments, a tricky goal, goes some way to explaining America's success at avoiding attack. It took Osama bin Laden nearly a decade to bring down the twin towers [the World Trade Center] after his organisation first tried in 1993. The vastness of the Atlantic and the Pacific also continue to provide some measure of safety. Brian Jenkins, a senior adviser at RAND, a think-tank, offers two more possibilities: the Muslim-American community seems to be inhospitable to violent extremism; and jihadists might not want to enrage a public that is tiring of America's commitments in Iraq and Afghanistan.

It is clear that American policymakers have not rendered the United States invulnerable to terrorist attack, particularly small-scale operations. There is little to stop a few extremists with machine guns from shooting up a mall, hurting American commerce briefly. Stopping more ambitious attacks, meanwhile, is still probably at least as much a matter of luck as of skill. So far, America has been blessed with a bit of both.

CHAPTER 2

Is the Department of Homeland Security Effective?

Chapter Preface

O ne of the most significant changes made by the U.S. government in response to the September 11, 2001, terrorist attacks was the creation of a massive new bureaucracy called the Department of Homeland Security (DHS). At the time of the attacks, no single federal agency was responsible for homeland defense, and analysis later revealed a serious lack of coordination between the various government entities then responsible for national defense, including the Federal Bureau of Investigation (FBI) and the Central Intelligence Agency (CIA). The idea, therefore, was to create a domestic counterpart to the Department of Defense (DOD), which is responsible for defending the country abroad, and place all the functions related to internal security in one Cabinet-level agency. Accomplishing this goal required the unprecedented merger of twenty-two federal agencies and almost 180,000 federal employees—the largest reorganization in the federal government since the DOD itself was created in 1947.

The process began less than a month after 9/11 (October 8, 2001), when President George W. Bush established the Office of Homeland Security (OHS), the precursor to DHS, to coordinate homeland security activities. The president appointed former Pennsylvania Governor Tom Ridge to head the office and charged him with formulating a comprehensive national strategy to secure the United States from terrorist threats or attacks. Today, the OHS is remembered mostly for the Homeland Security Advisory System, a color-coded terrorism risk-assessment system, which was used to issue terrorism alerts and to warn the public about potential terrorist attacks. The program was widely criticized for unnecessarily raising people's anxiety about the dangers of terrorism without providing any effective anti-terror advice.

On November 25, 2002, the OHS was merged into the DHS when the new agency was established by the Homeland Security Act of 2002. Tom Ridge assumed leadership of the DHS and became the nation's first Secretary of Homeland Security. The reorganization became effective on March 1, 2003, and all twenty-two agencies formally became part of DHS. Some of the diverse agencies merged into DHS included the Immigration and Naturalization Service (INS), which was responsible for immigration matters; the Federal Emergency Management Administration (FEMA), the nation's disaster response agency; the Customs Service, charged with keeping illegal drugs and products out of the country; and the Coast Guard, responsible for defending the nation's coastlines and waterways.

The DHS was structured around four major areas: border and transportation security; emergency preparedness and response; information analysis and infrastructure protection; and science and technology. FEMA and the Coast Guard have retained their identities as separate divisions within the new DHS structure, but numerous new directorates were created, including:

- United States Customs and Border Protection (CBP)—responsible for protecting our nation's borders and preventing terrorists and weapons from entering the United States;

- United States Citizenship and Immigration Services—responsible for the administration of immigration and naturalization functions and services;

- United States Immigration and Customs Enforcement (ICE)—responsible for enforcing the nation's immigration laws;

- The Transportation Security Administration (TSA)—responsible for protecting the country's transportation systems; and

- The Directorate for Science and Technology—a research and development arm responsible for providing federal, state, and local officials with the technology and capabilities needed to protect the nation.

Neither the FBI nor the CIA were folded into the DHS, despite the fact that some of the major failures in coordination before 9/11 were attributed to them. Nevertheless, President Bush praised the new federal department, noting that the agencies responsible for border, coastline, and transportation security would now be under one roof, and declared: "The continuing threat of terrorism, the threat of mass murder on our own soil, will [now] be met with a unified, effective response."

In the more than five years since its creation, the DHS has been credited with some successes. Most commentators agree that airport security has been tightened. Tens of thousands of new baggage screeners were hired; airplane cockpit doors were secured; and thousands of new air marshals now ride along anonymously on certain flights. Border and seaport security also have been improved. However, the agency has also received widespread criticism. Among other complaints, critics say that the creation of a huge bureaucracy has only hindered the nation's ability to respond to terrorist and disaster emergencies, and that DHS has already spent billions of federal funds on dubious pork barrel projects that have little to do with homeland security. DHS also is often attacked for failing to protect the nation's infrastructure, such as roads, bridges, ports, water systems, and chemical and nuclear facilities, as well as other likely terrorist targets.

More than five years after its creation, DHS is considered by most observers to be a work in progress. Yet defenders of the agency say the idea of a unified terrorist and disaster response system is still a good idea, and that more time is needed to get the system working smoothly. The authors in this chapter debate the question of DHS's effectiveness and offer opinions about which areas need improvement.

2007 Was a Year of Tremendous Progress and Maturation for the Department of Homeland Security

Michael Chertoff

Michael Chertoff is Secretary of Homeland Security and leads the U.S. Department of Homeland Security.

I am coming up on the third anniversary of my being sworn in as Secretary of Homeland Security, and we are at the end of another year of operations for the Department [of Homeland Security (DHS)]. . . . So I think this is a particularly good time to take stock of where we've been, what we've accomplished over the last year, what lessons we can draw from our experience, and to think about the challenges that lie ahead and how we are going to address them.

A Year of Progress

2007 was, in fact, a year of tremendous progress and maturation for this Department. From border security and immigration enforcement to passenger screening, critical infrastructure protection, and emergency response, we launched a number of important initiatives to strengthen our nation's security, and we began to see the fruits of our labor in a number of vital areas.

The year was not without its challenges. While there were no successful terrorist attacks here in the homeland, we did continue to face serious threats, including plots against Fort Dix, N.J. and JFK Airport [in New York City]. These plots

Michael Chertoff, "Remarks by Homeland Security Secretary Michael Chertoff on 2007 Achievements and 2008 Priorities," December 12, 2007. www.dhs.gov.

were disrupted by our partners and ourselves through sound intelligence, including, in one case, information provided by an alert citizen in N.J.; and all by working in partnership at the federal, state and local level, and with the private sector. . . .

Often, [DHS] accomplishments are unsung because they're quiet accomplishments, because we've avoided a problem.

We also saw record numbers of air travelers at our airports, including more than 17 million travelers during the week of Thanksgiving. Despite this high volume, and the continued and necessary restrictions on liquids in carry-on baggage, peak wait times at the busiest airports rarely exceeded 13 minutes—and in most places, were substantially lower. This, by the way, is a great non-story story. If there had been a lot of long lines and complaining passengers, I guarantee we would have seen a lot of news media attention. But there was comparatively little to the absence of complaining in long lines, and I think that's a tribute to our TSA [Transportation Security Administration] screening work force.

But it also underscores one of the challenges of this department, which is that often, accomplishments are unsung because they're quiet accomplishments, because we've avoided a problem rather than because we've embraced a problem. And therefore there's an extra challenge on us to make sure the people at DHS understand how much we appreciate the work they do, which often is in what they avert from happening as opposed to something affirmative that occurs. . . .

Now, I'm not going to tell you that we achieved perfection. No human effort is without error—and we had our share of errors this year—but we did learn, we matured, we challenged ourselves, and we grew stronger and more united as a department. And so, what I'm going to do in the next minutes is to take the opportunity to review some of our key accomplishments, particularly with regard to what I have often described as our five overarching goals. What are these goals—keeping dangerous people from entering the country; keeping dangerous goods from entering the county; protecting the critical infrastructure on which our lives and our economy depend; strengthening emergency response and building a culture of preparedness; and finally, improving the department's management.

Keeping Out Dangerous People

First, let me talk about protecting against dangerous people. What this really depends upon is having advance information about who's coming here, having the ability to quickly and accurately confirm the person's identity and to check him against watch lists, preventing the use of fraudulent documents, and determining who the unknown terrorist is; the terrorist whose name we haven't yet identified but who is nevertheless a real threat and someone that we ought to keep out.

We have made some very important strides to improve our ability to screen . . . travelers who come into the U.S.

Now this challenge is particularly remarkable when you consider that over the past year [2007], more than 414 million people came through our ports of entry. That means we literally had seconds to determine the level of risk of each one of these people. And we had to determine that level in a way that allowed the vast majority of innocent travelers to pass without hindrance, while making sure we didn't commit errors that would admit a terrorist or a serious criminal.

We have made some very important strides to improve our ability to screen these travelers who come into the U.S. Earlier this year, we reached a landmark agreement with our European counterparts to continue sharing advance information on passengers arriving and departing our country. . . .

[And] in order to improve our ability to confirm identity and check visitors against watch lists, this year we began taking 10 fingerprints. . . .

Because of our capability to take 10 fingerprints, and the collection of latent fingerprints from battlefields and training camps and safehouses, we now have a much enhanced capability to identify the unknown terrorist; the person whose name we don't have on a watch list, whose biographic information may not tip us off to the threat, but who has left a little piece of themselves somewhere and some place that suggests we ought to take a closer look. . . .

If we do have someone on a watch list, or we do know someone who's a criminal and shouldn't be admitted, then, of course, it's very important that we can ascertain they're not masquerading as somebody else. And so to close a known vulnerability, one identified by the 9/11 Commission—travel documents—we have initiated the Western Hemisphere Travel Initiative. This was passed by Congress. It reflected the 9/11 Commissions's observation that in the hands of a terrorist, a forged or stolen document is like a weapon. And what it requires is that we have only robust and secure documentation acceptable as a form of identification to allow you to enter the United States.

This year [2007] we arrested more than 3,500 illegal alien gang members and their associates.

As part of the Western Hemisphere Travel Initiative, this year we began requiring citizens of the U.S., Canada, Mexico and Bermuda to present a passport when arriving at our international airports. This closed a vulnerability that had existed, because people traveling from these locations with those citizenships had previously been allowed to appear with literally hundreds of different kinds of documents, which were very difficult to inspect and check for fraudulent nature or for their being counterfeit. . . .

This year [2007] we arrested more than 3,500 illegal alien gang members and their associates. ICE—Immigration and Customs Enforcement—added 23 new fugitive operations teams to identify and capture and deport illegal aliens who have defied a court order to leave the country. These teams arrested more than 30,000 fugitives—nearly double the arrests in the prior fiscal year.

Keeping Out Dangerous Goods

Now as I said, our mandate is not only to protect against dangerous people entering the country, but also dangerous goods, including, in particular, goods that might be radioactive, or other weapons of mass destruction. Our approach here is not to rely on any single layer of protection, but multiple layers of protection. . . .

Today we are scanning more than 97 percent of inbound cargo for radiation at our seaports.

So this year, we launched our Secure Freight Initiative at six overseas ports. This is designed to test our ability to scan 100 percent of inbound cargo for radiation before the cargo was loaded on a ship to come to the United States. This is part of pushing our defenses and our security outward, and it's an effort we undertake in partnership with our allies and friends overseas. . . .

Complementing Secure Freight overseas, we also expanded our Container Security Initiative [CSI] to 58 foreign ports. Here, again, using the tools I've described—the scanning and the intelligence-derived information—our inspectors now work with their foreign counterparts to screen cargo before it's loaded on to the ship. And with the current deployment, more than 85 percent of the containers shipped to the U.S. now transit through CSI ports and benefit from our overseas inspection.

With respect to our own ports of entry at our own border perimeter, we achieved a major milestone this year with . . . our . . . Radiation Portal Monitor. Today we are scanning more than 97 percent of inbound cargo for radiation at our seaports—over 90 percent at our northern border and 100 percent along our southern border. And next year, we will complete the job of getting pretty close to 100 percent at our northern border as well. All of these layers make our maritime domain safer and our land domain safer, in terms of shipping in goods. . . .

Protecting Infrastructure

Let me turn to the third element of what we have been accomplishing this year, and that is strengthening our domestic critical infrastructure. We used congressional authority that we received late in 2006 to implement tough, new chemical security regulations designed to protect chemical facilities from attack, and to prevent the theft of chemicals that could be used as weapons. As part of this effort, we work with the chemical industry to devise performance-based standards— not standards that give us the ability to micro-manage private business and tell them how to do their business, but rather, standards that set metrics and requirements, hold them accountable to meet those metrics and requirements, but allow them to devise the particular way in which they can best achieve those metrics and requirements without sacrificing the core of their business.

We also accelerated our IED [improvised explosive device] awareness campaign, boosted science and technology research into explosives, and expanded participation in our information-sharing portal to share expertise and raise awareness of the threat posed by IEDs.

At our seaports, we began enrolling port workers in our Transportation Worker Identification Credential program to protect our nation's airports and air travelers. We proposed new regulations that will allow TSA to take over the control of domestic passenger watch lists under our Secure Flight program. . . .

We not only have watch lists, we not only have the TSA screening function, but we are now deploying behavioral screening officers to more than 40 of our nation's airports in order to identify potentially threatening passengers based on their behavior. We've learned lessons, for example, from the Israelis and the Europeans in how to train our screeners to look for certain kinds of behavior that denotes a possible threat or an uneasiness that warrants a closer inspection. This is a proven tool. It enhances yet another layer of security, and it helps us build an element of randomness in the process, which is very important in terms of deterring terrorists. . . .

Emergency Response

Now let me turn to emergency response. As I've said, we are an all-hazards department, and heaven knows we've seen just about every kind of hazard you can see over the past few years. This year, as part of an effort since Hurricane Katrina to retool and transform FEMA [Federal Emergency Management Administration], we had the opportunity to test some of the developments in FEMA that we have put into place over the last 24 months, including better tracking of commodities, prearranged mission assignments with the Department of Defense that allow us to move more quickly to deploy Defense Department resources, and improved disaster registration. . . .

FEMA's employees are finally getting the tools and capabilities they have lacked for decades. As a result, FEMA's response time improved over the past year, and FEMA was praised for being on the scene quickly during the California fires, the tornadoes in Alabama and Kansas, and other disasters. And to make sure that state and local officials have the ability to communicate during a disaster, this year we awarded $1 billion in Public Safety Interoperable Communications grants and released interoperability scorecards for 75 urban areas in our country.

All of us have ... a stake in the success of this [Home-land Security] department, and a stake in the success of homeland security.

Integrating the Department

With all of this, the last area of accomplishment is in the integration and unification of this department. It's a young department, it's not even five years old, and we have to continue to work to integrate the core management functions and to achieve a cohesive and unified agency. . . .

We obviously will continue to listen and learn and grow as a department. We're going to work with Congress, and in a spirit of collaboration with our state and local partners and with the American people, because all of us have not only in an official capacity, but in a very personal capacity, a stake in the success of this department, and a stake in the success of homeland security.

The Department of Homeland Security Is Making Progress in Recruiting Veterans

Robert Brodsky

Robert Brodsky is a reporter for Government Executive, *a business news daily for federal managers and executives.*

The Homeland Security Department [DHS] has made significant progress in the hiring of veterans, but a wave of looming retirements across the federal sector could make future recruitment and retention difficult, a top House Democrat said [in November 2007]. . . .

On the heels of Veterans Day, the House Homeland Security Subcommittee on Management, Investigations and Oversight held a hearing examining DHS' efforts to recruit, hire and train veterans. Subcommittee Chairman Rep. Christopher Carney, D-Pa., said he was encouraged by steps the department has made in recent years to reach out to members of the armed forces for post-military employment. "While our committee has had countless hearings on DHS shortcomings, hiring of veterans at DHS is an area where the department seems to be on the right track," Carney said.

Veterans Hired by DHS

Among civilian agencies, DHS, along with the Transportation and Veterans Affairs departments, employs the highest percentage of veterans—nearly 40,500 as of [November 2007].

Marta Brito Perez, DHS' chief human capital officer, said that in fiscal 2007, DHS hired 6,013 veterans, nearly double the number from fiscal 2006 and more than four times the total from fiscal 2005. The Customs and Border Protection and Immigration and Customs Enforcement bureaus both nearly tripled the number of veterans on their payroll during the past year, while the Federal Emergency Management Administration doubled its numbers, Perez said. "We value the experience, commitment and work ethic that veterans bring to the job, as well as their significant skills and abilities," she said. "Their military backgrounds and training are well-suited for DHS jobs—and most important—to accomplishing our critical mission."

But Eric Hilleman, deputy director of the legislative affairs office for the Veterans of Foreign Wars of the United States, worries that DHS soon could become a victim of its own success. "With an increase of veteran applicants and wider recognition of DHS' desire to attract skilled applicants, the larger number of applications and inflow of paper will quickly inundate the small staff working on this initiative," Hilleman testified. "This overburdened staff will face the daunting task of placing these veterans within the numerous components within DHS." Hilleman urged the panel to provide a permanent funding stream to sustain many of the department's veteran recruitment programs.

It's of the utmost importance that DHS leverages [veterans'] experience, dedication and training to strengthen the department.

Carney sees other potential problems. He fears that a looming federal retirement wave—more than 60 percent of federal employees will be eligible to retire during the next decade, according to one recent estimate—could make recruitment more challenging as veterans find a wealth of opportunities available to them. "The department must do everything it can to stay competitive with other federal agencies when recruiting, retaining and promoting veterans," Carney said.

"Their unquestionable service ethic makes them ideal federal employees. It's of the utmost importance that DHS leverages their experience, dedication and training to strengthen the department."

Recruitment Efforts

Last week, DHS convened the first meeting of its Veterans Outreach Advisory Council, a group comprised of service organizations such as the American Legion, Veterans of Foreign Wars and Vietnam Veterans of America. The first of its kind in the federal government, the council will advise DHS on the effectiveness of its veterans outreach efforts, Perez said.

The department also has launched a Web site for veterans seeking employment with DHS. The site contains job postings, application requirements, an e-mail box for inquiries and submitting documents, and a converter to help veterans identify which positions best relate to their military specialties.

One of the more successful veterans outreach ventures has been Operation Warfighter, according to Leslye Arsht, deputy undersecretary of Defense for military community and family policy. Defense launched Operation Warfighter two years ago as a temporary-assignment program for soldiers recovering at military treatment facilities in the Washington region. The program matches service members with opportunities in the federal market that coincide with their interests and skills. Since 2006, 315 soldiers have been placed within 80 participating federal agencies and subcomponents, with an average posting ranging from three to five months. About 40 permanent job placements have resulted from program assignments following the service member's medical retirement, including 12 at DHS.

"Through this program, service members are able to build their résumés, explore employment interests, develop job skills and gain valuable federal government work experience to help prepare them for the future," Arsht said. "It has been our experience that, while these service members will no longer be in uniform, the large majority are still interested in serving their country in some capacity and see working for the federal government as an ideal solution."

The Department of Homeland Security Is Actively Engaged in the War on Terror

George W. Bush

George W. Bush was the 43rd president of the United States (2000–2008).

I'm very proud of the hard work of the men and women of the Homeland Security Department. This vital department is actively engaged in the war on terror. We are still a nation at risk. Part of our strategy, of course, is to stay on the offense against terrorists who would do us harm. In other words, it is important to defeat them overseas so we never have to face them here. Nevertheless, we recognize that we've got to be fully prepared here at the homeland.

Elements of the DHS Strategy

Part of that preparation requires a robust budget. We submitted the budget, you testified on the budget. It's about an 8 percent increase in the budget of the Homeland Security Department.

This department works to secure our borders. I appreciate very much ... [the] department's hard work of doing a difficult job, and that is doing what the American people expect and that is to have secure borders. But we're making good progress. We're modernizing a border that needed to be modernized, whether it be through fencing or the different types of high-tech investments.

I firmly believe that in order for your Border Patrol agents to be able to do their job, we need a guest worker program so that people don't have to sneak in our country, and therefore,

George W. Bush, "President Bush Discusses Department of Homeland Security Priorities," *The White House*, February 8, 2007. www.whitehouse.gov.

we can really enable your good folks to be able to focus on terrorism, drug runners, gun runners.

I appreciate so very much the fact that we've got a wise strategy to effect the security of our ports and cargo. We've got a lot of good people working hard overseas. In other words, we're inspecting cargo before it leaves a port—foreign port—so that the first line of defense is away from our shores, or away from our ports. And we've got a lot of good people working hard to achieve that.

I appreciate so very much the effort of TSA [Transportation Security Administration]. You've got a hard job. It's a job that really was a response to 9/11, and that is we don't want people getting on our airplanes that will terrorize our fellow citizens again. I fully recognize that there are thousands of hardworking people that are trying to do their best to, on the one hand, accommodate our fellow citizens as they travel; on the other hand, protect our country from attack.

We also talked about the need to have effective response if there is an emergency, if there is a catastrophe. And one agency that has been under fire and that needed to be reorganized was FEMA [Federal Emergency Management Administration] and I asked David Paulison to do just that. We took the lessons learned from Katrina and applied it to this vital agency. And this agency was recently tested through the tornadoes there in central Florida. And I want to thank you, Dave, and your team for a quick response to help the poor citizens who were affected by that natural disaster.

The Department of Homeland Security was initially melded together by organizations that tended to be stovepiped—independently run organizations that we felt needed to be brought under the central planning, the central organizing principle of a single department. The organization of such a vast enterprise has been difficult and complicated; nevertheless, there is noticeable and substantial and measurable progress.

And I appreciate all the hardworking folks for putting together an institute, part of our government, all aiming to protect the American people. . . . I oftentimes say to the American people that you can go about your business, you can run your enterprises, you can send your children to school, knowing full well that there are thousands of our fellow citizens who work every day, 24 hours, to help you by protecting this homeland. And this is where it all starts. And I thank you for your hard work.

The Department of Homeland Security Has Not Made Us Safer

Harris Sherline

Harris Sherline is a retired CPA from California who writes on a wide variety of topics.

For the most part, I have always been an optimist, generally seeing opportunity in difficult situations. But, I must admit that when it comes to homeland security, I tend to be somewhat pessimistic. When I do think about it, I invariably ask myself, Are we secure? Has our government done enough to make the American homeland safe? Are we doing enough ourselves, as individuals? Is it even possible to make us secure?

Starting with the fact that we are relatively new at this game having begun to focus intently on the problem only since 9/11, my sense is that it's a bit early to know just how secure we can be. But, one thing for sure, in my judgment, at this point we are definitely not secure. . . .

We are so plagued by political correctness that it prevents us from even doing something as basic as profiling airline passengers.

Holes in the Nation's Security

The Administration and many Republicans have been taking credit for the fact that we have not suffered another major terrorist attack since 9/11, which makes me wonder what the reaction of the American people will be when it finally happens. And, it is going to happen! Chances are, the reaction will be

Harris Sherline, "Is Our Homeland Secure?," *American Daughter*, June 4, 2007. Reproduced by permission. http://editorials.americandaughter.info.

to "throw the bums out." Unfortunately, that won't make much difference—because we will only get another bunch just like them in office.

Every time I hear the head of Homeland Security, Michael Chertoff, talk about what the government has done or is doing to protect America, I wonder how anyone can actually believe we are adequately protected when we are so plagued by political correctness that it prevents us from even doing something as basic as profiling airline passengers. Over five years after 9/11 we are still not inspecting most of the cargo on airplanes and at our ports, or adequately protecting our water and food supplies, power plants, etc. And, what about the potential of suicide bombers attacking our public places, such as major shopping malls? If anything would disrupt our way of life, that certainly would.

Our leaders responded to 9/11 by creating the largest bureaucracy in American history, the Department of Homeland Security.

A Huge Bureaucracy

Our leaders responded to 9/11 by creating the largest bureaucracy in American history, the Department of Homeland Security, with a $46.8 billion budget and upwards of 200,000 employees. Just looking at the organization chart is enough to boggle the mind: There are 22 departments organized in five levels of bureaucracy. The major agencies are Transportation Security, U.S. Customs & Border Protection, U.S. Citizenship & Immigration Services, U.S. Immigration Customs Enforcement, U.S. Secret Service, Federal Emergency Management Agency (FEMA) and the U.S. Coast Guard. They all report to the Secretary of Homeland Security, along with 18 other assorted Secretaries, Officers, Directors and the like. There is also a Homeland Security Advisory Council, which provides advice and makes recommendations to the Secretary of Homeland Security.

To my eye, it looks like an organizational nightmare, with a span of control that exceeds the ability of any single individual to manage. Just looking at it raises questions. And, as usual, Congress has a hand in managing everything, adding to the complexity and confusion that surrounds the agency's activities.

Without adequate border security there can be no homeland security.

In my opinion we are a long way from being secure. I also believe we can never be completely safe. How on earth is it possible for us to protect ourselves from every conceivable attempt to attack us, ranging from nuclear to poisoning our food and water, to attacking our transportation systems (air, shipping, railroads, trucking), power grids, major installations and Lord knows what else? One thing for sure, without adequate border security there can be no homeland security. Listening to the endless arguments about securing our borders, especially with Mexico, it is obvious that we are wide open to being infiltrated by our enemies.

Protecting Citizens

Apart from 9/11, the breathtaking scope of the Katrina disaster underscored the fact that the most important function of government is to protect its citizens. So, what are we getting for our $46.8 billion Homeland Security budget, especially at the local level?

For the most part, it's a top down system, with the agencies that comprise the Department of Homeland Security applying their funding to a wide variety of programs, including emergency preparedness activities at the state and county levels. But, in spite of this, are we really prepared for major emergencies, such as fires, torrential rains, accidents involving hazardous materials, earthquakes or other natural disasters—and the unthinkable, a terrorist attack or perhaps the overflow consequences of one in a major metropolitan area?

When there is a fire, earthquake, tornado, flood, who's available to help? We tend to rely on local fire, police or sheriff's departments, public utilities, agencies like the Red Cross, or the National Guard. But, what if no one can get to you for two or three days, or a week? What can you do? Are you adequately prepared to tough it out on your own? New Orleans vividly demonstrated that most people are not.

In a major crisis, the reality is that you will probably have to fend for yourself until help arrives, conceivably days, a week, or longer.

Protecting Ourselves

In a major crisis, the reality is that you will probably have to fend for yourself until help arrives, conceivably days, a week, or longer. There are simply not enough police, firefighters and emergency personnel to respond to every situation.

Think about how unprepared you probably are for an emergency. Everything from fire extinguishers to first aid kits and CPR [cardiopulmonary resuscitation] training to an adequate supply of food and water to a pre-determined survival plan and escape route for your family, to just plain knowing what to do to protect your home and loved ones and to help your neighbors.

Thomas Sowell [a syndicated columnist and senior fellow at the Hoover Institute] made the following observations in an article about New Orleans and Katrina: "When all is said and done, government is ultimately just human beings—politicians, judges, bureaucrats. Maybe the reason we are so often disappointed with them is that they have over-promised and we have been gullible enough to believe them."

Government cannot solve all our problems, even in normal times, much less during a catastrophe of nature that reminds man how little he is, despite all his big talk. The most basic function of government, maintaining law and order, breaks down when floods or blackouts paralyze the system. During good times or bad, the police cannot police everybody. They can at best control a small segment of society. The vast majority of people have to control themselves.

If we don't know what to do in a major emergency, and we expect our local police and firefighters to be the first responders, and they are not available, who will be accountable: the federal Department of Homeland Security, the state government, your city council or county board of supervisors? As we have already seen with Katrina in New Orleans, there will be plenty of blame to go around.

In the final analysis, self-help is inescapable. Think about it. Are you prepared? Do you know what to do if outside help cannot get to you when the next major emergency strikes, which will surely happen?

There's another major emergency in your future, and the likelihood that the government, local, state or federal, will be able prevent it or provide 100 percent protection is slim to none. We all need to be prepared to take care of ourselves and to help our neighbors until the situation stabilizes.

A 2007 General Accounting Office Report Gives the Department of Homeland Security a Failing Grade

Government Security

Government Security magazine covers technological advances in homeland security, as well as issues of procurement and trends in all aspects of government security.

A new progress report on implementation of mission and management functions of the Department of Homeland Security from the Government Accountability Office (GAO) has been released to lawmakers. It reports that, according to the GAO, the Department of Homeland Security (DHS) shows inadequate funding, unclear priorities, continuing reorganizations and the absence of an overarching strategy. The report marks the sixth anniversary of Sept. 11, 2001, as the Democratic Congress, Republican White House and presidential candidates from both parties are beginning to debate the administration's record of accomplishments since that date.

The GAO Findings

The GAO states that after the largest government merger in more than half a century, the DHS met fewer than half of its performance objectives, or 78 of 171 directives identified by President [George W.] Bush, Congress and the department's own strategic plans. The department strongly disputes the report.

In one of its harshest conclusions, the 320-page document states that the DHS has made the least progress toward some of the fundamental goals identified after the 2001 attacks and

Government Security, "Progress Report Marks Six-Year Anniversary of Sept. 11," September 6, 2007. Reproduced by permission.

again after Hurricane Katrina in August 2005: improving emergency preparedness; capitalizing on the nation's wealth and scientific prowess through "Manhattan project"-style research initiatives; and eliminating bureaucratic and technical barriers to information-sharing.

[Homeland Security] Secretary Michael Chertoff . . . [said] the Bush administration . . . deserves credit for the absence of another strike on U.S. soil.

Senate Homeland Security Committee Chairman Joseph I. Lieberman (I-Conn.) said that although the DHS "has made important progress," it requires more focused attention and money. "Clearly, we have a long way to go before the department achieves the goals we set out for it four and a half years ago," said Lieberman, who will chair a hearing on the matter this week.

At a hearing before the House Homeland Security Committee, Secretary Michael Chertoff sought to preempt the GAO's findings, saying the Bush administration has "unequivocally" made the nation safer since 2001 and deserves credit for the absence of another strike on U.S. soil. At the time, "no one would have been bold enough to predict that six years would pass without a further successful attack on the Homeland," Chertoff said. He also complained that Congress itself has failed to streamline its oversight of the DHS, according to *The Washington Post*.

An Ineffective Agency

Analysts from across the political spectrum have complained that the DHS has spent $241 billion over four years without performing a disciplined analysis of threats and implications.

The GAO report draws on more than 400 earlier reviews and 700 recommendations by congressional investigators and the department's inspector general, as well as the goals set by the Sept. 11 commission, the Century Foundation, congressional legislation and spending bills, and the administration's own plans and internal strategic documents, such as the White House's National Strategy for Homeland Security from July 2002.

GAO analysts acknowledged that DHS's enormous size and complexity—spanning 220,000 employees and 22 component agencies—make the challenge "especially daunting and important." They also said they do not intend to suggest that the DHS should have already met all expectations. "Successful transformations of large organizations, even those faced with less strenuous reorganizations than DHS, can take at least five to seven years to achieve," the GAO stated, as reported in *The Washington Post*.

Still, although prior studies focused on the DHS's many organizational problems—leading Chertoff to direct the department to sharpen its focus after he took office in February 2005—the report indicates that it still has difficulty carrying out policy decisions and setting priorities.

The DHS met only five of 24 criteria for emergency preparedness, failing to implement a national response plan or develop a program to improve emergency radio communications. The department met just one of six science and technology goals, such as developing research and development plans and assessing emerging threats; and two of 15 computer integration targets, the report says.

Moderate progress, which the GAO defined as taking action on more than half of identified goals, was made in only five of 14 areas—immigration enforcement; aviation, land and transportation security; securing critical facilities such as bridges, power plants and computer networks; and property management—and substantial progress in just one, maritime and port security.

The Department of Homeland Security Has Not Taken a Strategic Approach

Daniel Byman

Daniel Byman is director of the Center for Peace and Security Studies at Georgetown University and a senior fellow at the Saban Center for Middle East Policy at the Brookings Institution.

Once again, the Department of Homeland Security [DHS] is in the cross hairs. A just-released Government Accountability Office [GAO] report bashed DHS for making limited progress on emergency-response capabilities and the management of human capital. DHS's progress was rated as "substantial" in only one of the 14 areas surveyed: maritime security. Although the GAO's criticisms are valid, it measures homeland security by bureaucratic-efficiency standards rather than by whether our country is safer from a terrorist attack. The report and other critiques of DHS miss the broader problem: The U.S. government has not taken a strategic approach toward homeland security.

A Lack of a Strategic Approach

The lack of a strategic approach has led to several real risks and vulnerabilities that go beyond the scope of the GAO report. Perhaps most important, DHS does not focus on ensuring the support of American Muslims. If terrorists can hide among a sympathetic local community, the job of police and intelligence officials is daunting. On the other hand, if locals oppose terrorism, the radicals must constantly be on the run. As the recent arrests in Germany suggest, homegrown terrorists, particularly those aided by skilled foreigners, can pose a grave danger. Fortunately, in contrast to Europe, American Muslims are well-integrated, well-educated, and prosperous, and many local law-enforcement officials are having more success reaching out to this community. Many breaks in much-trumpeted FBI successes against supposed jihadists at home, such as the case of the "Lackawanna Six," have come from local community members calling in tips.

Still, this goodwill should not be taken for granted. A 2005 survey of Muslim youth activists found that 70 percent felt that the American public had "significant hostility" toward Muslims. This is not paranoia on the part of young Muslims. Racist comments directed at Muslims have become more frequent since 9/11, as have acts of intimidation, such as the vandalism of mosques.

No Focus on Perceptions

A second strategic problem is that no government agency focuses on perception management (though DHS technically has a mandate for part of this mission). In Israel, after a terror attack, special crews rapidly clean up the scene in order to signal that terrorism will not disrupt daily activity. In the United States, in contrast, government officials inadvertently send the opposite message. Then-Department of Health and Human Services Secretary Tommy Thompson's 2004 declaration that "I cannot understand why the terrorists have not, you know, attacked our food supply because it is so easy to do" is perhaps a particularly low point in public rhetoric, but in general our leaders seem to delight in emphasizing potential vulnerabilities, often showing an imagination far beyond that of actual terrorist groups.

Terrorist use of a radiological "dirty bomb"—a real possibility—illustrates this problem. An attack and the ensuing radiation poisoning would likely kill only a few people, but many more casualties would result if frightened people were to race out of town because the government was unable to reassure them that they would be safe if they remained.

While the FBI has made many strides since 9/11 ... the bureau still has significant problems in how it recruits, hires, and develops its leaders.

Inadequate Domestic Intelligence

Domestic intelligence is another strategic challenge. The FBI [Federal Bureau of Investigation] is outside the Department of Homeland Security's purview, yet it remains perhaps the most important agency with regard to domestic security. Historically, the FBI's strength has been law enforcement, not intelligence. While the FBI has made many strides since 9/11, a report by the National Academy of Public Administration found that the bureau still has significant problems in how it recruits, hires, and develops its leaders.

Thomas Kean and Lee Hamilton, who co-chaired the 9/11 Commission, reported [in September 2007] that analysts are still second-class citizens in the bureau. Because the FBI does not regularly produce a domestic threat assessment, U.S. policy-makers still do not have a comprehensive view of the current threat (or lack thereof) and how it is evolving. The "first responders"—state and local officials—often lack access to intelligence and are out of the loop.

Understanding Terrorists

U.S. officials also need to integrate a better understanding of its adversaries into the nation's defenses. Terrorists seek targets that will resonate with their constituents. We should ask what will play in Peshawar, Pakistan, not Peoria, Ill. Despite Thompson's fears, planning for a massive agro-terrorism event would be wasteful if al-Qaida or its affiliates have no intention of laying waste to the U.S. corn crop. The United States has spent billions on port security, yet, to our knowledge, no jihadist group has ever devised a serious attack plan for such a strike. As these criticisms suggest, better security doesn't require spending more on defending even more potential targets. Clark Kent Ervin, the former inspector general at the Department of Homeland Security, warns that terrorists could attack shopping malls, movie theaters, restaurants, nightclubs, and similar soft targets and, in so doing, "terrorize the entire nation." Perhaps. But at the same time, Ervin notes that terrorism is "like water, it seeks, finds, and takes the path of least resistance." Ironically, such a statement also argues *against* protection.

Excess preparation for homeland security can waste tens or hundreds of billions of dollars that could be better spent on fighting terrorists abroad.

In theory, we could guard every restaurant, nightclub, gas station, or for that matter, any place where people congregate. But even if all public places were protected, the terrorists could simply shoot the guards and proceed with their attack. In practice, we can't protect everything, and we must remember that terrorists have their own priorities that lead them to concentrate on a limited set of targets.

It is tempting to say that too much preparation never hurts and that a steady drumbeat of fear is necessary to prepare for what is, in the end, a dangerous movement. After all, who wouldn't drive a car that was "too safe" or eat a diet that was "too healthy"? But excess preparation for homeland security can waste tens or hundreds of billions of dollars that could be better spent on fighting terrorists abroad, or, for that matter, on health care, auto safety, or a tax cut. Aside from the dollars wasted, many of the proposed defensive measures could impede trade, discourage tourism, and restrict civil liberties.

The very concept of homeland security is new for Americans, and the department was thrown together quickly and involved many already-dysfunctional bureaucracies. Even so, our nation's dialogue on homeland security is disappointing. Mistakes, misconceptions, and a lack of strategic thinking are tolerable in the immediate aftermath of an unprecedented terrorist attack like 9/11, but they are less forgivable six years later.

Congress Has Created More Bureaucracy but Less Security for Americans

Ron Paul

Ron Paul is a member of the U.S. House of Representatives from Texas who has run as a Republican candidate for president.

Congress voted [in May 2007] to authorize nearly $40 billion for the Department of Homeland Security, but the result will likely continue to be more bureaucracy and less security for Americans.

We can only wonder whether we are more vulnerable than we were before Homeland Security was created.

Five years into this new department, Congress still cannot agree on how to handle the mega-bureaucracy it created, which means there has been no effective oversight of the department. While Congress remains in disarray over how to fund and oversee the department, we can only wonder whether we are more vulnerable than we were before Homeland Security was created.

More Bureaucracy, Less Security

I was opposed to the creation of a new Homeland Security department from the beginning. Only in Washington would anyone call the creation of an additional layer of bureaucracy on top of already bloated bureaucracies "streamlining." Only in Washington would anyone believe that a bigger, more centralized federal government means more efficiency.

When Congress voted to create the Homeland Security department, I strongly urged that—at the least—FEMA [Federal

Ron Paul, "More Bureaucracy, Less Security," antiwar.com, May 15, 2007. Reproduced by permission of the author.

Emergency Management Administration] and the Coast Guard should remain independent entities outside the department. Our Coast Guard has an important mission—to protect us from external threats—and in my view it is dangerous to experiment with rearranging the deck chairs when the United States is vulnerable to attack. As I said at the time, "the Coast Guard and its mission are very important to the Texas Gulf Coast, and I don't want that mission relegated to the back burner in a huge bureaucracy."

We are spending more money and getting less for it with the Department of Homeland Security.

Likewise with FEMA. At the time of the creation of the Department of Homeland Security, I wrote "we risk seeing FEMA become less responsive as part of DHS. FEMA needs to be a flexible, locally focused, hands-on agency that helps people quickly after a disaster." Unfortunately and tragically, we all know very well what happened in 2005 with Hurricanes Katrina and Rita. We know that FEMA's handing of the disaster did in many cases more harm than good. FEMA was so disorganized and incompetent in its management of the 2005 hurricanes that one can only wonder how much the internal disarray in the Department of Homeland Security may have contributed to that mismanagement.

Folding responsibility for defending our borders into the Department of Homeland Security was also a bad idea, as we have come to see. The test is simple: We just ask ourselves whether our immigration enforcement has gotten better or worse since functions were transferred into this super bureaucracy. Are our borders being more effectively defended against those who would enter our country illegally? I don't think so.

Are we better off with an enormous conglomerate of government agencies that purports to keep us safe? Certainly we are spending more money and getting less for it with the Department of Homeland Security. Perhaps now that the rush to expand government in response to the attacks of 9/11 is over, we can take a good look at what is working, what is making us safer, and what is not. If so, we will likely conclude that the Department of Homeland Security is too costly, too bloated, and too bureaucratic. Hopefully, then we will refocus our efforts on an approach that doesn't see more federal bureaucracy in Washington as the best way to secure the rest of the nation.

CHAPTER 3

What Measures Should Be Taken to Enhance Homeland Security?

Chapter Preface

Part of the definition of the term "homeland security," and part of the job of the Department of Homeland Security (DHS), involves responding to natural disasters, such as hurricanes, tornadoes, fires, and floods. Prior to the creation of DHS, this responsibility resided with the Federal Emergency Management Administration (FEMA)—an agency that is now part of DHS. Although FEMA once was considered highly effective, its performance has been widely criticized since it was absorbed by DHS.

During the 1990s, FEMA established a reputation as one of the best-run federal agencies. Following the suggestions of a report published by the General Accounting Office (GAO) in 1992, then-incoming president Bill Clinton changed the mission of FEMA, from providing relief during a nuclear attack to responding with emergency aid during natural disasters. Clinton appointed James Lee Witt as the agency's director, and Witt assembled a formidable and competent new staff, reorganized the agency to function more effectively, and beefed up programs designed to help prepare states for natural disasters, such as floods, fires, hurricanes, and tornadoes. These changes eliminated bureaucratic delays and provided FEMA with the ability to respond rapidly to disasters, often within a matter of hours.

During the next decade, FEMA responded to several emergencies and disasters, earning praise for its performance each time. In 1993, for example, when floods in the Midwest threatened to collapse a water plant and cut off water supplies to residents of Des Moines, Iowa, a call to a FEMA disaster field office brought immediate assistance in the form of water purification machines that provided clean water until the facility could be restored. And in 1995, when a truck bomb exploded and destroyed a federal office building in downtown Oklahoma City, a FEMA team arrived on site within hours of receiving a phone call for help from the state. These and other efforts earned FEMA commendations from Congress and from state disaster officials throughout the country.

After FEMA was merged into DHS as part of the George W. Bush administration's response to 9/11, however, the agency appeared to deteriorate. FEMA and DHS faced their first big challenge in 2005, when Hurricane Katrina flooded New Orleans and wiped out a vast stretch of the gulf coastline of Louisiana, Mississippi, and Alabama. Katrina killed almost twelve hundred people, left more than a million homeless and displaced, and caused tens of billions in property and economic losses. Many called it the worst natural disaster in the nation's history. FEMA's response, however, was almost universally condemned as being late, incompetent, and ineffective. Following lengthy congressional hearings in 2006 on FEMA's performance during Katrina, the Senate Homeland Security and Governmental Affairs Committee even called for completely abolishing the agency. The Bush administration rejected this advice and DHS officials instead promised to improve FEMA.

FEMA faced an opportunity to repair its damaged image in 2007, when wildfires broke out in five southern California counties, forcing half a million people to evacuate and destroying nearly 2,200 homes. Although difficult, this fire emergency was much smaller than the Katrina disaster, which by comparison damaged or destroyed roughly 500,000 homes and caused severe and widespread damage to infrastructure and communications systems. This time, FEMA crews arrived in California even before President Bush had declared a national disaster. Federal FEMA workers set up temporary offices at San Diego's Qualcomm Stadium, where many evacuees were housed during and after the fires, and within a week FEMA began issuing grants up to $28,800 to fire victims. Although there have been some complaints about a lack of trailers for use as temporary housing, many commentators gave FEMA good marks for its response to the 2007 fires.

Despite some improvements within FEMA, many experts say that more changes are needed to ensure that the federal government adequately responds to the types of human-generated and natural disasters likely to face the United States in the 21st century. One proposal is to update the Robert T. Stafford Disaster Relief and Emergency Assistance Act—the law that authorizes federal disaster assistance to residents, businesses, and governments after the president declares a "major disaster." Critics have said that the current law was written to deal with smaller scale disasters and that it is inadequate for catastrophes like Hurricane Katrina. In the case of Katrina, for example, where New Orleans was forced to lay off half its workforce because it had no ability to manage or pay them, the Act authorized assistance to pay for overtime work of local emergency workers but not to pay these regular salaries. The Act also caps cash assistance to affected households at $28,800, and only authorizes this after victims show proof of insurance coverage. Experts say funds could be authorized immediately to victims of major catastrophes, allowing people to immediately begin rebuilding and to repay the government later after insurance proceeds are received. The need for further reform and improvement at FEMA is especially needed, critics say, because climate experts are predicting many more intense weather events as a result of global warming—making it likely that FEMA will encounter more catastrophic disaster challenges in the future.

Improving the nation's disaster response, however, is just one of many suggestions being made for enhancing the country's homeland security. The authors in this chapter offer a number of different proposals that touch on various security-related programs.

Congress Should Concentrate on Five Basic Areas to Fix Homeland Security

James Jay Carafano

James Jay Carafano is assistant director of the Kathryn and Shelby Cullom Davis Institute for International Studies and a senior research fellow for National Security and Homeland Security in the Douglas and Sarah Allison Center for Foreign Policy Studies at The Heritage Foundation, a public policy think tank.

The task of homeland security is to help keep America safe, free, and prosperous. Congress plays an important role in achieving these goals. By any measure, 2007 was not the best year for homeland security in Congress. Its landmark legislation for the year, the "Improving America's Security by Implementing Unfinished Recommendations of the 9/11 Commission Act of 2007," did anything but what its title promised, adding numerous unnecessary mandates that were never mentioned by the Commission. At the same time, Congress left unfixed homeland security faults that have lingered for years. Congress can do better in the new year by sticking to five New Year's resolutions that fix the errors it introduced in 2007 and address long-time oversights.

Congress has failed to consolidate jurisdiction of the [Homeland Security] department under one committee in each chamber as recommended by the 9/11 Commission.

---

1. Consolidate congressional oversight of the Department of Homeland Security. Congress has failed to consolidate jurisdic-

James Jay Carafano, "Homeland Security: Five New Year's Resolutions for Congress," *Heritage Foundation*, WebMemo #1763, December 31, 2007. Reproduced by permission. www.heritage.org.

tion of the department [of Homeland Security] under one committee in each chamber as recommended by the 9/11 Commission. DHS [Department of Homeland Security] officials report to a plethora of committees that offer conflicting and competing guidance. Committees continue to tinker with the department, moving offices and adding missions; committees other than the homeland security committees still retain jurisdiction over major parts of the department, including the Coast Guard. Consolidating jurisdiction in a single committee in each chamber will resolve these and other coordination problems.

[Congress should] stop turning homeland security grants into "pork-barrel" funding.

---

2. *Stop turning homeland security grants into "pork-barrel" funding.* The 9/11 Commission warned about this problem, and 2007's 9/11 Commission Act made things worse. Though the bill reduces the minimum in homeland security grants that must go to each state from 0.75 to 0.375 percent of the total, it applies that minimum to other grant programs as well, which had never been done before. This change is an enormous step backwards, fencing off even more money for each state (regardless of its need) than before. Based on authorized funding levels, the change will give each state a minimum of $6,750,000, which is $200,000 more than the smallest states received in 2007. Congress should eliminate all minimums and insist that all funds be allocated based on national priorities. Congress should also eliminate grants which contribute little to national homeland security, such as Assistance to Firefighter Grants.

3. *Establish an undersecretary for Homeland Security.* Since DHS was created, many have come to recognize that the agency needs a high-level, high-powered office to develop policies that bind the more than 22 federal entities consoli-

dated within the department, to coordinate with other federal agencies, and to manage international affairs for the department. Congress has yet to authorize an undersecretary for the department to supervise these activities.

4. *Repeal the requirement for 100-percent scanning of all shipping containers bound for the United States.* Congress mandated 100-percent scanning in the 9/11 Commission Act, despite the fact that the 9/11 Commission rejected this proposal. No congressional mandate is more intrusive, expensive, and unnecessary. Inspecting every container that is shipped to the U.S. makes no sense. Doing so would cost billions of dollars and drown authorities in useless information. Moreover, it is not clear why every container would require inspection. The "nuke-in-a-box" scenarios deployed to justify such drastic measures are highly implausible. Scanning and sealing every container will not make Americans much safer but will increase the cost of just about everything that American consumers buy. Already, the United States evaluates every container coming into the country and inspects the suspicious ones. It is not a perfect system—it can be improved—but it is a reasonable precaution and deterrent. One-hundred percent inspection is not.

5. *Finish immigration and border security reform.* Congress must let DHS move forward with border security and internal enforcement initiatives. This includes changing the law to allow the sharing of Social Security "no-match" data with DHS so that the department can track down employers who regularly hire large numbers of unlawfully present workers. In addition, Congress should move forward on visa reform and improve visa services so that employers can legitimately get the workers they need to grow the economy.

Congress has much to do to improve on its below-par performance on homeland security in 2007. These five priorities are good places to start.

Following Our Basic Values Is the Foundation for Our Security

Brian Michael Jenkins

Brian Michael Jenkins is a senior adviser for the RAND Corporation. The following viewpoint is taken from Jenkins's testimony presented before the House Appropriations Committee, Subcommittee on Homeland Security, on January 30, 2007.

Homeland security is not a television show about mysterious government agencies, covert military units, or heroes with fantastic cell phones that summon F-16s. It is an ongoing construction project that builds upon philosophy and strategy to ensure effective organization, establish rules and procedures, deploy new technology, and educate a vast army of federal agents, local police, part-time soldiers, private security guards, first responders, medical personnel, public health officials, and individual citizens. Homeland security is about national commitment in general and the distribution of resources in particular, and therefore, it is about legislation and appropriations.

Enduring Tasks

Homeland security is not over in 24 hours. Providing for the common defense and protecting the homeland—the principal tasks of government—have become the challenge of our generation. Our projects must be durable, our efforts sustainable. Failures will be obvious, but it will be hard to know when we get it right. Villains will not visibly bite the dust by the end of

Brian Michael Jenkins, "Basic Principles for Homeland Security," Testimony Before the Committee on Appropriations, Subcommittee on Homeland Security, House of Representatives, January 31, 2007. © 2007 RAND. Republished with permission of RAND Corporation, conveyed through Copyright Clearance Center, Inc. www.rand.org.

each episode. Absence of a major attack does not automatically mean that security is effective, but it can tempt us into dangerous complacency.

The terrorist threat is changing. We have degraded the global operational capabilities of al Qaeda, removed some of its key planners, and kept its leadership on the run. But we have not prevented jihadist leaders from communicating, blunted their message, or effectively countered their ability to radicalize and recruit angry young men. Our attention must shift to local conspiracies, which may operate below our intelligence radar. This increases the importance of domestic intelligence-collection and the role of local police.

[Ensuring homeland security means] implementing security regimes that are consistent with American values and traditions.

The dynamic nature of the threat precludes us from ever saying, "Mission accomplished." Combating terrorism and ensuring homeland security are enduring tasks. That does not mean accepting the notion of perpetual war. It does mean formulating a sustainable strategy and implementing security regimes that are consistent with American values and traditions, that do not impede our economy, that build upon our strengths as a nation rather than magnifying our fears.

We can develop security measures that are compatible with our basic freedom.

Basic Principles

How we translate this lofty rhetoric into specific decisions about the distribution of precious resources is your task as elected officials and members of the Appropriations Committee. There are no recipes. But there are some basic principles.

- Security must be defined broadly to include all efforts to deter, detect, prevent, and impede terrorist attacks; mitigate casualties, damage and disruption; reduce alarm; and rapidly respond, repair, and recover.

- Intelligence capabilities must be improved at the local level. We are slowly moving in this direction, but local governments face competing demands and are strapped for resources. Subsidizing the construction of intelligence fusion centers does not by itself create intelligence capability. That requires manpower and training, which also require continued support, and equally important, a less bureaucratic approach to the ownership of intelligence information.

- We need to examine our legal framework for preventive action, which differs from routine reactive criminal investigation. Broad assertions of executive authority are not a long-term solution in a society of laws.

- A more proactive approach means that mistakes inevitably will be made and, therefore, must be accompanied by comprehensive oversight and the means for prompt remedy.

- We confront a wide array of potential terrorist scenarios, each one of which will be championed by a determined, well-informed, and vocal advocate with the result that all seem equally dangerous. But we must beware of unwittingly transforming vulnerabilities into imminent terrorist threats. Vulnerabilities are infinite. Choices must be made.

- Terrorists can attack anything, anywhere, any time. But we cannot protect everything, everywhere, all the time. So security will necessarily be reactive. This is not a cause for blame when an attack occurs. It does not mean we are fighting the last war when we subsequently implement measures to prevent easy repetition of the attack. But it should not provoke overreaction.

- Allocations of resources must be based upon assessments of risk—we are moving in this direction. The choice lies between focusing on the most likely events in the lower registers of violence or on the less likely events that would have the greatest consequences. Current U.S. strategy is moving toward disaster-driven.

- If we are thinking about terrorist disasters, we urgently need to address how we can do a better job of post-disaster recovery. Our terrorist foes talk about crippling our economy with devastating attacks. No enemy of the United States should think that a city or a region can be put out of business. The sad neglect of the Gulf Coast creates exactly that impression.

- Security and liberty are not exchangeable currencies. We can develop security measures that are compatible with our basic freedom. But that freedom can be imperiled by attempts to eliminate all risk.

- Prevention of all terrorist attacks is an unrealistic goal. It cannot be the criterion for assessing the effectiveness of security measures. Our goals are to deter terrorist attacks, improve our chances of detection, increase the terrorists' operational difficulties, drive them toward less lucrative targets.

- Although we do it every day, living with risk is a hard political sell, which is why our efforts should include educating the public, helping citizens realistically assess the terrorist perils and everyday dangers they face, making them savvy about how security works and its limitations. We must inculcate a security culture without creating a security-obsessed state.

- Given the great uncertainty about the terrorist threat, which we cannot abolish, we should favor those projects that offer dual or collateral benefits. Improving our crisis-management capabilities and strengthening our public-health infrastructure are examples. Investments then will not be wasted even if no terrorist attack occurs.

- Where feasible, the emphasis should be on the development of capability at the local level rather than the expansion of federal programs. Obviously, this will not be appropriate for the security of our national borders, airlines, or nuclear facilities, or for other large tasks, which must remain federal responsibilities.

- New initiatives should offer a net security benefit—that is, any measure proposed should do more than merely displace the risk from one target set to another, unless the second-choice targets are less lucrative.

- Strict cost-benefit analysis will not work. Terrorist attacks are infrequent but potentially disastrous events, and while direct security costs can be readily calculated, the consequences of a large-scale terrorist attack—those beyond casualties and damage—cannot so easily be quantified.

- Security must be both effective and efficient. We have already seen that security measures can have insidious effects on the economy. New security proposals should be accompanied by some estimate of long-term costs, impact on the basic function of what is being protected, effect on civil liberties, and other collateral effects.

- We are a nation of inventors. Technology can increase the effectiveness of security measures and streamline security procedures. Creativity should be encouraged—

that means risking some research failures. New systems should be rapidly deployed for testing in the field, with successful systems disseminated nationwide. This dynamic process depends on defining the capabilities we want to achieve within certain time limits, not on national uniformity of devices or machines. We should not wait for a silver bullet.

- The ability of technology to reduce manpower requirements is less certain. New systems require trained human operators and continued quality control and testing, something we often overlook in budgeting. For the next ten to fifteen years, security, like intelligence, will remain manpower-intensive. There are no "hands-free" security solutions.

- Homeland security can be a basis for rebuilding America's aging infrastructure. We can build things that are more robust—inherently hard targets—build in redundancies to mitigate the consequences of failure, design for resiliency and rapid recovery. It means not isolating security concerns from functional considerations. There may be ways to improve security without increasing long-term security costs.

- In order to focus limited security resources, we must be able to employ selective methods: systems that fast-track identified travelers, the latest versions of computer-assisted passenger screening, selective searches based upon observed behavior. Since this runs contrary to the public's preference for security that is passive and egalitarian, it must be accompanied by public education. Success depends on cooperation in an environment of trust, which, frankly, has been eroded by government overreach and cavalier dismissal of traditional guarantees.

- Homeland security must aim to counter both the terrorists and the terror they hope to create—the event and its psychological impact. We can achieve this by increasing public education and participation. This is far more than reminding people to be vigilant. Individual, family, and community preparedness should be a national goal, with everyone playing a part. Knowledge and specific responsibilities are the most effective shields against terror. Here, participation, not effectiveness, is the objective. I might add here that if the American people believe this struggle requires no sacrifice from them and will not support leaders who acknowledge this need, then we have a very big problem. I am optimistic, but I don't have to run for office every two years.

- We are a nation of volunteers and should build on that tradition. Legislation has been introduced to create a Civilian Reserve Corps. The President mentioned it in his [2007] State of the Union message. It is a good idea, but why confine the idea to American nation-building efforts abroad. A domestic Civilian Reserve Corps could be a way of matching skills volunteered with skills needed in case of natural or man-made disaster. The readiness of citizens to help one another in times of danger and crisis remains one of the great untapped strengths of this nation of 300 million people.

Prevention of all terrorist attacks is an unrealistic goal.

In the final analysis, homeland security is not guaranteed by concrete barriers or more guards. As I have written in my recent book, *Unconquerable Nation*, I believe that this nation will remain unconquerable as long as we adhere to our basic values—our love of liberty and justice, our strong sense of community, our courage, our self-confidence, our tradition of self-reliance. These are the foundation of our security.

The United States Must Continue to Improve Its Domestic Intelligence System

David Heyman

David Heyman is a director and senior fellow for the Homeland Security Program at the Center for Strategic and International Studies (CSIS), a think tank in Washington, D.C.

A steady stream of stories [are] cropping up about government collection of information on Americans in the fight against terrorism. In each case, the story sparks controversy and the Administration defends the actions as legal, necessary, and not unduly intrusive. But these assurances do not relieve public unease about a growing domestic role for national security agencies that traditionally have focused their attentions outward.

Of all the issues that we have wrestled with since 9/11, perhaps none has received more consideration or attention in discussions on homeland security than the acknowledged shortcomings of intelligence—in collection, analysis, and sharing—prior to the September 2001 attacks. In the United States, intelligence collection is split between agencies that look outside of our borders (e.g., the military, the Central Intelligence Agency [CIA]) and those that look inward (the Federal Bureau of Investigation [FBI]). And while there has been significant attention paid to the reorganization, revitalization and resourcing of our foreign intelligence services, far less attention has been paid to the domestic side of the equation.

There is, however, a clear new need and many new activities emerging to bolster intelligence capabilities to support post-9/11 homeland security/defense missions. And yet the in-

David Heyman, *Threats at Our Threshold*, Washington, DC: Center for Strategic & International Studies, 2008. Reproduced by permission. www.csis.org.

crease in domestic intelligence (DI) collection has moved forward with little public discussion, no apparent framework, and little oversight. This raises the prospect of an emerging domestic intelligence 'system' where all the pieces don't fit together, pieces are missing or redundant, and there is no framework for protecting individual liberties. To address DI responsibly requires answering fundamental questions about what agencies should be responsible for collecting intelligence within the United States; what types of domestic information the government should collect, and how it should be used; and how the government needs to coordinate and oversee the process to assure effectiveness and protection of civil liberties.

The Need for Domestic Intelligence

Increased focus on DI is a necessary response to the threat posed by international terrorism. Terrorists live, work, plan, and act all over the world, including within our borders. They move and communicate with relative ease between foreign capitals and U.S. cities. The 9/11 attacks represent a failure of intelligence agencies—foreign and domestic—to communicate and coordinate as the planners and perpetrators lived within and traveled in and out of the United States for months prior to the attack, with little notice.

Countering threats abroad cannot substitute for strengthening protection at home.

Despite our success in Afghanistan, eliminating a regime that had provided safe haven for terrorists to train and launch operations to attack us, terrorism has neither been quelled nor conquered. To the contrary, terrorist recruitment and terrorist attacks continue to expand. Homegrown terrorism is on the rise in Europe, Australia, and North America, and the spread of radical Islamist ideology has hastened, gaining traction in fragile democratic states from Lebanon to Indonesia.

Countering threats abroad cannot substitute for strengthening protection at home. We must be able to anticipate, prepare for, and interdict attacks at home. Because the threat at home is greater now than during the Cold War, when we worried more about attacks from nation-states abroad than from non-state attackers on American soil, confronting this threat requires greater understanding of domestic information and more flexibility in sharing analysis, and the use of that information.

Emerging Elements of Domestic Intelligence

To address the much-recognized need for intelligence reform following the 9/11 attacks, the U.S. government instituted a series of some of the most sweeping reforms of the nation's intelligence apparatus since the end of World War II. Among the changes following the 2001 attacks are the creation of new organizations, new missions, and new positions. They include:

- Establishment of the Homeland Security Council (HSC) at the White House to coordinate all homeland security–related activities among executive departments (including related-intelligence); and specifically, setting-up a Homeland Security Policy Coordination Committee (HSC/PCC) for the expressed purpose of coordinating interagency policy on detection, surveillance, and intelligence.

- Establishment of a new homeland defense mission for the U.S. military, a new Northern Command (USNORTHCOM) responsible for providing command and control of Department of Defense (DoD) homeland defense and civil support efforts, and a new Assistant Secretary of Defense for Homeland Defense (ASD/ HLD) to provide homeland defense related guidance for USNORTHCOM. Both ASD/HLD and USNORTH COM will require intelligence to perform their duties to protect America at home.

- Formation of a new National Security Branch (NSB) at the FBI to protect the United States against weapons of mass destruction, terrorist attacks, foreign intelligence operations, and espionage.

- Creation of an Undersecretary for Intelligence at DoD charged with integrating defense intelligence, surveillance, and reconnaissance capabilities to better provide warnings, actionable intelligence and counter-intelligence support necessary for national and homeland.

- Establishment of a new Assistant Secretary for Information Assurance and Infrastructure Protection at the Department of Homeland Security (DHS) (transformed today to Assistant Secretary for Intelligence and Analysis) to identify and assess current and future threats to the homeland, map those threats against our current vulnerabilities, inform the President, issue timely warnings, and immediately take or effect appropriate preventive and protective action.

- Induction of the U.S. Coast Guard—responsible for protecting U.S. economic and security interests in any maritime region including America's coasts, ports, and inland waterways—into the U.S. intelligence community and establishment of the Coast Guard Intelligence Coordination Center as its primary interface with the collection, production, and dissemination elements of the national intelligence and law enforcement communities.

- Creation of the National Terrorist Threat Integration Center (now the National Counterterrorism Center or NCTC), an interagency body intended "to provide a comprehensive, all-source-based picture of potential terrorist threats to U.S. interests."

- Consolidation of all U.S. intelligence functions and activities to be coordinated under a newly created Director for National Intelligence (DNI).

The approach to initiating and implementing DI reforms, however, has been ad hoc, fragmented and has emerged without a strategic vision to follow. In October 2005, the new Office of the Director of National Intelligence (ODNI) issued its blueprint for building "an integrated intelligence capability to address threats to the homeland, consistent with U.S. laws and the protection of privacy and civil liberties." Despite this effort, the document failed to develop specific roles and missions, clear rules for collection, or how information should be shared among intelligence partners and other associated homeland security stakeholders.

In a world where non-state actors can gain asymmetric advantage by operating within the gaps of a dysfunctional or inefficient bureaucracy, one of our goals must be to deny terrorists safe harbors in the seams of society—seams between foreign and domestic, civil and military, federal and state, public and private, and even agency to agency—but to do so while also ensuring that we uphold the pillars that are at the heart of America's constitutional identity—federalism, liberty, and justice. This requirement raises complex legal and policy issues because by its nature, DI collection affects the privacy and civil liberties of U.S. citizens and residents.

On the civil liberties side, an undefined, potentially unlimited program of covert surveillance of the American public raises huge privacy concerns.

Problems in the Absence of a Domestic Intelligence Framework

If there is no framework for DI, no clarity about roles and responsibilities in its collection, each agency will set out on its own to get what it needs. Such activities can have negative consequences not only for civil liberties, but also for effectiveness. On the civil liberties side, an undefined, potentially unlimited program of covert surveillance of the American public raises huge privacy concerns, both in perception and in practice. In terms of effectiveness, when collection roles overlap or are not clearly defined, there is great risk that players will trip over each other by pursuing the same leads or sources, or will miss something because they believe others will pursue it. These or other mishaps could compromise important and sensitive activities.

The world of intelligence is largely closed. As a consequence, public debate is often limited between those who are uninformed or poorly informed. Those who have the facts are constrained by secrecy requirements from discussing the details, or, in some cases, even the broad outlines of the activities. Those who 'know' can stymie public discourse with arguments that any discussion would telegraph the nature or details of government collection to our enemies. Those that 'don't know' can inspire public fear and diminish public confidence by imagining the worst.

The [George W.] Bush Administration and its national security officials have generally shied away from any broad discussion of how they will address the increased need for domestic intelligence. In his confirmation hearings, the new DNI, Michael McConnell, stated that the Intelligence Community has been "trained for years to think external, foreign," but stressed that with the terrorist threat it is important to "think domestically." The ODNI, however, has so far been reluctant to take responsibility for setting a policy framework for collection and use of domestic intelligence. This leaves each agency to make its own judgments about what information it needs and how to get it.

When it comes to discussing this issue, outside of the government, experts have tended to focus primarily on an organizational question: should the FBI remain the country's DI agency or should we separate the intelligence and law enforcement functions and create the U.S. equivalent of MI-5, the United Kingdom's domestic intelligence service. This is an important question, but it is not the only question, and it should not be the first. What is most important is for the government to create a consistent and clear framework for its collection and use of DI.

The Nation Must Develop a Legal Framework for Detaining Terrorist Suspects

Benjamin Wittes and Mark Gitenstein

Benjamin Wittes is fellow and research director in public law at the Brookings Institution, as well as a columnist for the New Republic Online, *a political and culture magazine. Mark Gitenstein is a nonresident senior fellow at the Brookings Institution.*

Six years after the September 11 attacks, the United States still lacks a stable, legislatively established policy for detaining suspected foreign fighters captured in the war on terrorism. American detention policy has eroded this country's international prestige and public image, embroiled its military in continuous litigation, and cast a pall of legal uncertainty and impropriety over the detention of several hundred suspected enemy fighters. . . .

[A long-term detention] system [must] be crafted in statutory law, thereby reflecting the considered judgment of the Congress of the United States—not merely the unilateral will of the executive branch or the judiciary's response to executive policy. As the Supreme Court has pointed out on several occasions, government decisions are most credible when all three branches agree.

Developing rules for detaining suspected enemies engaged in unconventional warfare . . . represents the core challenge facing American legal policy in the war on terrorism.

Developing rules for detaining suspected enemies engaged in unconventional warfare against the United States and its in-

Benjamin Wittes and Mark Gitenstein, "A Legal Framework for Detaining Terrorists: Enact a Law to End the Clash over Rights," *The Brookings Institution*, November 15, 2007. Reproduced by permission. www.brookings.edu.

terests represents the core challenge facing American legal policy in the war on terrorism today. The next President should work with Congress to assure that those rules conform to constitutional principles and fundamental American values, are as widely accepted as possible both domestically and abroad, and buttress rather than undermine the global campaign against terrorism and extremism.

The Debate over Detentions

Debate among presidential candidates, opinion leaders, foreign policy experts, and judicial commentators over the treatment of Al Qa'eda and Taliban fighters—so called "unlawful enemy combatants"—has been extensive and spirited, but unfortunately it has avoided the core of the problem: *what U.S. policy toward detaining foreign combatants should be.*

For several years, the detention debate has been playing out in the federal court system and in Congress. . . . The origin of the debate was a series of executive actions by the [George W.] Bush Administration to create special detention procedures and facilities, including a detention center at Guantanamo Bay Naval Base in Cuba. These actions prompted rebukes by the Supreme Court, which, in turn, have led so far to two rounds of legislation: the Detainee Treatment Act of 2005 [DTA] and the Military Commissions Act of 2006 [MCA].

The DTA followed two Supreme Court decisions handed down in June 2004: *Hamdi v. Rumsfeld*, an 8-1 decision in which the Supreme Court held that detainees who are U.S. citizens are entitled to certain procedural rights; and *Rasul v. Bush*, a 6-3 decision holding that the Guantanamo Bay facility does not lie, as the administration had contended, beyond the jurisdiction of the federal courts. In addition to addressing jurisdiction, the DTA also contained a provision sponsored by Senator John McCain (R-Ariz.), requiring that interrogations of detainees by the military at Guantanamo Bay and elsewhere conform to techniques prescribed in the Army Field Manual, thus precluding inhumane methods.

The MCA came in response to the 2006 *Hamdan v. Rumsfeld* decision, in which the Supreme Court decided 5-3 that the military commissions established by the administration violated the Uniform Code of Military Justice [a U.S. military code governing prisoners of war] and the Geneva Convention [an international treaty governing treatment of prisoners of war] on the treatment of enemy combatants. The MCA establishes procedures for using military commissions to try detainees for war crimes. Both the DTA and the MCA seek to erase the jurisdiction the Court had asserted to hear *habeas corpus* [a petition challenging detention] cases brought by or on behalf of detainees—a subject the Court will again take up in the current term [2008].

The Administration's Position

The Bush Administration has correctly insisted on the authority to detain foreign fighters outside of the four corners of the American criminal justice system. The current conflict has enough in common with traditional warfare to warrant giving the executive branch a detention authority, based in part on the power to hold enemy soldiers in a conventional military conflict.

The administration has taken this analogy too far, however. The war on terrorism is not a conventional war. Too much factual uncertainty attends the status of individual detainees to permit their long-term detention based on procedures created solely by the executive branch and lacking in basic fairness to the accused, who may face a lifetime of incarceration. The proper detention regime for the war on terrorism is a hybrid of different legal structures, drawing on elements of the laws of war and the criminal law and tailored to the unique threat posed by global catastrophic terrorism. The system should produce decisions that have credibility both with the American public, to preserve support for the broader effort to combat terrorism, and with foreign audiences, to bolster support for—rather than zealous opposition to—American antiterrorism policy. . . .

The detention of [terrorist] fighters presents difficult questions to a democracy.

Balancing Civil Liberties and Wartime Needs

The detention of Taliban and Al Qa'eda fighters presents difficult questions to a democracy that values civil liberties and the rule of law yet wishes to prevail in a long-term conflict with irregular forces of extreme violence. Indefinite detention, even of non-citizens, runs counter to foundational notions of what this country stands for. The conflict between basic American values and indefinite detention energizes, as it should, the controversy over *habeas corpus* rights of detainees at Guantanamo.

But, the issue is complicated. Our legal system tolerates indefinite detention for a number of purposes, including protecting the U.S. population from aliens the government does not wish to admit but who cannot be returned home, preventing the dangerously mentally ill or sexually deviant from injuring people in the community, and isolating individuals with potentially fatal communicable diseases. Further, the concept that foreign fighters can be held indefinitely during times of war is incontrovertibly established in international and constitutional law. The Third Geneva Convention [an international treaty on the treatment of prisoners of war] specifically authorizes and regulates the detention of uniformed military captives, who can lawfully be kept off the field of battle for the duration of hostilities.

Terrorists Are a Unique Case

The problem is that the Guantanamo detainees, whom the administration terms "unlawful enemy combatants," do not fall within the Geneva Convention definition of "prisoners of war." They are not members of a uniformed army with a clear hierarchy of command. Rather, like saboteurs, they infiltrate the civilian community and engage in violence against noncombatants—activity that often meets the definition of "war crimes." Such forces, under the laws of war, are also subject to detention for the duration of the hostilities, assuming they can be identified; but they forfeit the generous protections afforded to POWs.

The administration argues that the Geneva protections should not extend to fighters who have no intention of reciprocating. Taliban and Al Qa'eda, after all, do not apply those rights to their detainees, whom they have been known to behead. In almost every way, rather, they flout the rules of warfare—at great peril to civilians.

The United States' refusal to give such people the protections due to prisoners of war is not new. Although President [Jimmy] Carter submitted to the Senate a protocol to the Third Geneva Convention that would have treated many members of terrorist groups as prisoners of war, the [Ronald] Reagan Administration withdrew the protocol, arguing that this erosion of the line between honorable soldiers and terrorists "would endanger civilians among whom terrorists and other irregulars attempt to conceal themselves." The *New York Times* and *Washington Post*, among others, sided with the Reagan Administration.

The paradox is that, precisely because terrorists flout the rules of warfare and make themselves harder to distinguish from civilians when captured, they necessitate a level of due process that conventional forces, which make no secret of their status as belligerents, do not require. The question is what sort of process might identify these unlawful combatants accurately and with public credibility. The Geneva Conventions require only that, in cases of doubt, all individuals receive review by a "competent tribunal"—historically, cursory field panels that provide few procedural protections. But such panels are a bad fit with the war on terrorism. In many of these cases, the factual issues are too complicated, the lines between civilian and combatant too hazy, the duration of the conflict too uncertain, and the consequences to the liberty of individuals too vast.

Congress therefore needs to create new statutory procedures for handling "unlawful enemy combatants" of the Guantanamo type. The procedures must not be subject to the whim of the executive. Instead, they should be blessed by all three branches of government, reflecting the unified will of the American political system. These processes need not include all the protections of a criminal trial. But, they need to be considerably more robust than the process applied to prisoners in a conventional military conflict or the process applied to detainees today at Guantanamo.

Defining Combatants

The threshold question for Congress is how to define the universe of people subject to detention. At a minimum, this group includes overseas fighters who are not members of any uniformed military but have engaged in hostilities against the United States or its allies. It also should include individuals who have purposefully planned, or knowingly and materially supported, those hostilities.

It is important to exclude individuals taken into custody within the United States or in Iraq or any other theater of war where the United States applies the Geneva Conventions to detentions, either by law or policy. The new process should be limited to the types of individuals currently in custody at Guantanamo—that is, long-term detainees held as part of the global conflict with Al Qa'eda and its affiliates.

Assuring Due Process Protections

This detention system will not have all the attributes of the criminal justice system, but it must have some, and it must create an adversarial process whereby detainees have a meaningful opportunity to dispute and contest the evidence against them. Key elements should include the following new features:

- *Impartial finder of fact.* The presiding officer should be a judicial officer, either a military or civilian judge.

- *Right to counsel.* The detainee should be represented by competent military counsel.

- *Access to evidence.* Counsel for the detainee should be able to see the evidence against his or her client, including classified information and all exculpatory materials. And, the detainee personally should be given a summary of the prosecution's evidence, specific enough to allow a fair opportunity to respond to it.

- *Full and fair hearing.* The detainee should be able to present evidence, obtain witnesses, compel testimony, cross-examine government witnesses, and respond to the government's evidence admitted against him.

- *Exclusion of illegally obtained evidence.* The law should bar the tribunals from considering statements obtained by torture or conduct just short of it.

- *Findings of fact and conclusions of law.* The process should result in a reasoned, written document that explains the detention judgment and is subject to review by the civilian courts of the United States.

- *Periodic review.* Some form of ongoing status review must ensure both that the continued detention of each enemy combatant is necessary and that the conditions of confinement are humane and lawful. Review decisions should be subject to appeal, but judicial review should be deferential. Detainees should have help in the process from their lawyers. And, the review process ought to be codified in law.

- *Habeas corpus.* Habeas review should indeed be preserved for detainees. It should, however, be applied as it is in criminal cases today—only after the process is complete and with considerable deference to the judgments that precede it. . . .

As a practical matter, the United States has no alternative to some form of administrative detention.

Time for Congress to Act

As a practical matter, the United States has no alternative to some form of administrative detention. Numerous detainees now at Guantanamo—and those likely to be captured in future—cannot realistically be put on trial, either because they have not committed crimes or because the main body of evidence is, for one reason or another, inadmissible. These people, however, may be too dangerous to set free. Across a number of areas of law—mental illness, warfare, immigration—the courts have approved carefully crafted schemes that permit non-criminal detentions in order to protect the public. The war on terrorism requires its own scheme, tailored to its particularities.

The Bush Administration's insistence on deriving this scheme purely from the laws of war, without involving the other branches of government, has resulted in a confused, widely criticized, poorly justified, and sometimes unfair system for which Congress has so far needed to take no responsibility. It is long past time for Congress to take ownership of this problem and to create the rules—rules that both authorize detentions and put limits on them—that will govern Guantanamo or whatever facility replaces it.

The U.S. Government Should Improve Its Emergency Preparedness System

E.L. Gaston is a 2007 graduate of Harvard Law School.

The [George W.] Bush Administration often asserts that the rules changed after September 11. As Cofer Black, the onetime director of the CIA's [Central Intelligence Agency] counterterrorism unit, testified to Congress in early 2002, "There was a before-9/11 and an after-9/11.... After 9/11 the gloves came off." While this has certainly been true on the law enforcement and intelligence side of the war on terror, the federal government has failed to reexamine the role it should play in responding to terrorist attacks and other public health and safety crises. On the contrary, despite increased funding and new institutional resources (including the Department of Homeland Security), the federal government continues to work within the pre-September 11 state-centered legal framework, preventing it from implementing the ambitious post-September 11 agenda it developed. Restrictions on federal involvement have contributed to systematic weaknesses including uneven implementation of national priorities, "unfunded mandates," poor information flows between the different levels of government, and poor coordination during actual crisis periods. It is time for the gloves to come off on homeland security. Federalism preferences must take a backseat to the country's immediate need for a functional preparedness and response system. . . .

E.L. Gaston, "Taking the Gloves Off Homeland Security: Rethinking the Federalism Framework for Responding to Domestic Emergencies," *Harvard Law & Policy Review*, vol. 1, July 20, 2007, pp. 519–532. Reproduced by permission. www.hlpronline.com.

Taking the Gloves Off of Counterterrorism

In response to September 11, Bush Administration officials set an ambitious counterterrorism agenda and then stretched the legal framework to enable the federal government to carry out those goals. As a result, the legal framework for federal law enforcement, intelligence, and detention capabilities has changed dramatically. The scope of these legal reforms demonstrates the Bush Administration's willingness to question formal restraints on its counterterrorism powers—in stark contrast to its approach to disaster preparedness and response.

After September 11, the Administration shifted from [a] law enforcement framework to a war paradigm.

The Bush Administration's willingness to challenge legal restraints on federal authority to arrest, detain, and interrogate terrorism suspects illustrates its functional approach to counterterrorism. Before September 11, the government investigated, detained, and prosecuted terrorism suspects. After September 11, the Administration shifted from this law enforcement framework to a war paradigm, arguing that constitutional and statutory limitations did not apply to "unlawful combatants" in the war on terror. Officials further argued that the President's commander-in-chief powers over detention, together with Congressional authorization to use all "necessary and appropriate" force against those responsible for the September 11 attacks, gave the federal government sufficient authority to detain individuals (including U.S. citizens) as enemy combatants and to hold them indefinitely without access to judicial processes or constitutionally guaranteed civil liberties. The Administration also declared that Common Article III of the Geneva Conventions [an international treaty governing prisoners of war] did not apply to members of Al Qaeda or the Taliban. It engaged in potentially cruel and inhumane means of interrogation, established secret detention facilities, and used extraordinary rendition to send detainees to countries that engage in torture, all in contravention of U.S. treaty obligations. It also tried to place combatants outside of Article III review and created military commissions without Congressional authorization despite the existence of contradictory Supreme Court precedent. Although the Supreme Court and Congress ultimately forced the Administration to abide by some international and domestic legal restrictions, the basic wartime detention model has been accepted.

The Administration has also pushed the boundaries on traditional domestic intelligence and law enforcement capabilities. It led Congress to relax law enforcement standards and restrictions on search and seizure through the USA PATRIOT Act in ways that scholars have argued "gutted" Fourth and Fifth Amendment rights. It expanded the use of secret and un-reviewable National Security Letters (NSLs) to demand private financial records of citizens in ways that compromise First and Fourth Amendment rights. It authorized National Security Agency (NSA) officials to engage in warrantless wiretapping of thousands of phone and internet exchanges of persons inside the United States, in violation of Supreme Court interpretations of Fourth and Fifth Amendment rights and also Foreign Intelligence Surveillance Act restrictions that were reaffirmed by Congress while the unlawful wiretapping program was ongoing. As with the detention and treatment of unlawful combatants, the Bush Administration defended its provocative actions by arguing that the nation should accept a wartime legal paradigm.

These examples demonstrate the degree to which the Bush Administration has attempted to reshape legal norms to meet the new demands of the war on terror. Despite heavy criticism by liberal legal scholars and some pushback from the other branches in the last two years, the Administration's hyperfunctional approach to defending the nation against terrorism has been largely acquiesced to by Congress, the Supreme Court, and the American people since September 11.

The Administration has been either unwilling or unable to reshape legal rules to improve intergovernmental response to the next terrorist attack.

Putting Form Above Function in Homeland Preparedness

In contrast to its gloves-off approach to counterterrorism, the Bush Administration has continued to put form over function in the realm of homeland preparedness and response. Nine days after the attacks on New York and Washington, D.C., President Bush announced a new initiative to "take defensive measures against terrorism" at home and to coordinate "at the highest level" the "dozens of federal departments and agencies, as well as state and local governments [with] ... responsibilities affecting homeland security." A new department was created to manage homeland security, and funding for homeland preparedness increased significantly. Yet pre-September 11 legal restrictions ... have continued to limit the federal government's efforts to improve the country's homeland security preparedness and response systems. Despite the Bush Administration's success at pushing legal boundaries in the fields of law enforcement and detention, in the area of homeland security the Administration has been either unwilling or unable to reshape legal rules to improve intergovernmental response to the next terrorist attack or crisis situation.

The Tenth Amendment [of the U.S. Constitution] reserves to the states many of the legal powers that would be useful in preparing for and responding to a terrorist attack or natural disaster. In a crisis situation, state officials alone would have the authority to enforce an intrastate quarantine, command the National Guard to enforce order, and commandeer intrastate resources, including means of transportation, shelter locations, and medical facilities. States have the responsibility to develop emergency resources and contingency planning with limited federal funding and some voluntary cooperation with the Federal Emergency Management Agency (FEMA). Upon request by a state, the President may declare a national disaster or national emergency under the Stafford Act, triggering emergency funding assistance. The Stafford Act also permits federal agencies to direct *federal* resources toward emergency response measures (including search and rescue, medical assistance, or supply and logistics efforts). In practice, however, federal agencies have a limited number of personnel to deploy because of the Posse Comitatus Act [a federal statute limiting the use of the military for state law enforcement].

These constitutional and statutory restrictions have created a culture of deference within the federal homeland preparedness and response community. According to Richard Falkenrath, former homeland security policy adviser to President Bush, "[T]he basic federal compact . . . is that the state and local agencies are responsible for disaster relief and management, and the federal government is just there to help as asked." Because local input and expertise are so critical to crisis response and because preparedness has traditionally fallen under the umbrella of state public health and safety, there is a strong presumption that crisis preparedness and response are state responsibilities.

Given its aggressively functionalist approach to deterring and preventing future terrorist acts, the Administration might have been expected to challenge this traditional deference where necessary to carry out its post–September 11 commitment to improving homeland preparedness. Instead, the Administration has accepted the restrictions imposed by federalism [the government system that gives states certain powers] preferences and consequently has worked within the existing state-centered framework. The only compulsory federal regulation enacted since September 11 was the National Incident

Management System (NIMS)—the much-derided color-coded system of threat warnings. According to Falkenrath, despite awareness that the emergency response system was "inadequate," the Bush Administration was too focused on other priorities to truly rethink the basic federal-state division of authority.

If anything, the Bush Administration has resisted legal or institutional reforms that would have enabled more aggressive federal action, and it has embraced federalism restrictions that limit its authority. President Bush's original plan envisioned a leanly staffed White House Homeland Security office to manage existing agency activities. The President proposed a cabinet-level department only after extreme public and Congressional pressure to do so. Even after the Department of Homeland Security (DHS) was created, top Administration officials emphasized the department's respect for existing federalism restrictions and deference to local authorities. The National Strategy for Homeland Security states, "[W]e should work carefully to ensure that newly crafted federal laws do not preempt state law unnecessarily or overly federalize counterterrorism efforts." Secretary Tom Ridge proudly proclaimed that DHS had "redefined a new federalism" with such initiatives as weekly conference calls with state directors and voluntary regulations on private businesses.

Congressional legislation has also reinforced the current state-centered framework. The Homeland Security Act of 2002, which created DHS, set broad goals for the agency to direct and coordinate state and local response systems along national homeland security priorities, but gave it little legal authority to do so. For example, Section 201 directed DHS to develop "a comprehensive national plan," specific measures that federal and state officials should take, information-sharing mechanisms, and to coordinate state-level training and support. Among the Act's nineteen enumerated goals, however, not one grants DHS the power to mandate that federal or state officials take the recommended information-sharing, emergency preparedness, or infrastructure-building measures. . . .

The federal government must be willing to take on more of the burden for implementing necessary crisis preparedness and response.

Taking the Gloves Off of Crisis Response

To achieve the more ambitious goals declared after September 11 and Hurricane Katrina, the federal government must be willing to take on more of the burden for implementing necessary crisis preparedness and response. Greater federal involvement during non-crisis periods would help ensure that preparedness priorities are implemented more consistently, and would allow federal actors to develop the working relationships with state and local actors necessary to assist effectively during a crisis.

As the above discussion of federalism restrictions suggests, expanding the federal role in crisis response may require relaxing or getting around formal legal restraints. The Supreme Court has held that the Constitution prohibits the federal government from commandeering or directing state legislatures or state executives to implement federal programs, even if states consented to the legislation ex ante [beforehand]. [Supreme Court] Justice [Antonin] Scalia's majority opinion in *Printz v. United States* rejected a balancing test that would have weighed the importance of the federal interest advanced, instead creating a bright-line "no commandeering" rule. Any reform that smacked of commandeering might be challenged as unconstitutional, although this Supreme Court has been willing to give the Administration broader latitude to reshape traditional legal frameworks in response to the exigencies of the war on terror. In addition, some scholars suggest that the authority to respond to domestic emergencies is not completely reserved to the states under the Constitution.

Regardless of whether the Supreme Court relaxes its anti-commandeering standards, the federal government could assume greater responsibility if it was willing to challenge some of the informal preferences for federalism. Other federal agencies, such as the Department of Commerce and the Department of Energy, project their influence through nationwide field offices. Federal employees in these departments work with state and local officials and private sector actors on a daily basis, encouraging voluntary adoption of agency priorities. After September 11, the FBI increased the size and capabilities of its Joint Terrorism Task Forces (JTTF), which are FBI-led field offices that facilitate counter-terrorism information sharing among state and local law enforcement officers, FBI Agents, and other federal agents. Having a field office presence is particularly appropriate for a department like DHS, whose mission is focused on the particular needs of, and threats to, state and local communities. Stronger local, state, and regional field offices also might be able to reinforce regional plans such as state mutual assistance compacts, and facilitate the deployment of available regional resources to the affected areas in times of crisis.

To be better prepared for the next homeland security emergency, the federal government needs to . . . remove outdated federalism restraints.

Policy proposals that increase federal involvement in local preparedness and response may face resistance by those who believe in a "small government" model of DHS. There is a common misperception that the importance of local knowledge to a successful preparedness and response operation makes any increase in federal involvement bad policy. The recognition that local control is critical in this area should not prevent an honest reconsideration of whether the current federalism balance is the best for implementing the government's goals. A better framework would retain the value of local input while relieving burdens on local actors by giving the federal government a greater capacity to implement the broader goals it has set.

Despite the increased funding and institutional resources that were provided after September 11, the current system remains sub par. As the disastrous response to Hurricane Katrina illustrated, a state-centered framework simply does not produce the level of governmental assistance that Americans expect or deserve in a crisis situation. The federal government should re-adjust the basic federal-state framework to reflect the new post–September 11 demands. To be better prepared for the next homeland security emergency, the federal government needs to do more than just channel funding through the existing flawed framework for crisis management: it needs to take the gloves off and remove outdated federalism restraints.

The Public Must Refuse to Be Terrorized

Bruce Schneier

Bruce Schneier is a security technologist and author.

On Aug. 16 [2006], two men were escorted off a plane headed for Manchester, England, because some passengers thought they looked either Asian or Middle Eastern, might have been talking Arabic, wore leather jackets, and looked at their watches—and the passengers refused to fly with them on board. The men were questioned for several hours and then released.

On Aug. 15 [2006], an entire airport terminal was evacuated because someone's cosmetics triggered a false positive for explosives. The same day, a Muslim man was removed from an airplane in Denver for reciting prayers. The Transportation Security Administration [TSA] decided that the flight crew overreacted, but he still had to spend the night in Denver before flying home the next day. The next day, a Port of Seattle terminal was evacuated because a couple of dogs gave a false alarm for explosives.

On Aug. 19 [2006], a plane made an emergency landing in Tampa, Florida, after the crew became suspicious because two of the lavatory doors were locked. The plane was searched, but nothing was found. Meanwhile, a man who tampered with a bathroom smoke detector on a flight to San Antonio was cleared of terrorism, but only after having his house searched.

On Aug. 16 [2006], a woman suffered a panic attack and became violent on a flight from London to Washington, so the plane was escorted to the Boston airport by fighter jets.

"The woman was carrying hand cream and matches but was not a terrorist threat," said the TSA spokesman after the incident.

And on Aug. 18 [2006], a plane flying from London to Egypt made an emergency landing in Italy when someone found a bomb threat scrawled on an air sickness bag. Nothing was found on the plane, and no one knows how long the note was on board. . . .

The point of terrorism is to cause terror, sometimes to further a political goal and sometimes out of sheer hatred. The people terrorists kill are not the targets; they are collateral damage. And blowing up planes, trains, markets or buses is not the goal; those are just tactics.

The point of terrorism is to cause terror, sometimes to further a political goal and sometimes out of sheer hatred.

The real targets of terrorism are the rest of us: the billions of us who are not killed but are terrorized because of the killing. The real point of terrorism is not the act itself, but our reaction to the act. And we're doing exactly what the terrorists want.

We're all a little jumpy after the recent arrest of 23 terror suspects in Great Britain. The men were reportedly plotting a liquid-explosive attack on airplanes, and both the press and politicians have been trumpeting the story ever since. In truth, it's doubtful that their plan would have succeeded; chemists have been debunking the idea since it became public. Certainly the suspects were a long way off from trying: None had bought airline tickets, and some didn't even have passports. Regardless of the threat, from the would-be bombers' perspective, the explosives and planes were merely tactics. Their goal was to cause terror, and in that they've succeeded.

Imagine for a moment what would have happened if they had blown up 10 planes. There would be canceled flights, chaos at airports, bans on carry-on luggage, world leaders talking tough new security measures, political posturing and all sorts of false alarms as jittery people panicked. To a lesser degree, that's basically what's happening right now.

The Danger of False Alarms

Our politicians help the terrorists every time they use fear as a campaign tactic. The press helps every time it writes scare stories about the plot and the threat. And if we're terrified, and we share that fear, we help. All of these actions intensify and repeat the terrorists' actions, and increase the effects of their terror. . . .

The implausible plots and false alarms actually hurt us in two ways. Not only do they increase the level of fear, but they also waste time and resources that could be better spent fighting the real threats and increasing actual security. I'll bet the terrorists are laughing at us.

The surest defense against terrorism is to refuse to be terrorized.

Another thought experiment: Imagine for a moment that the British government arrested the 23 suspects without fanfare. Imagine that the TSA and its European counterparts didn't engage in pointless airline-security measures like banning liquids. And imagine that the press didn't write about it endlessly, and that the politicians didn't use the event to remind us all how scared we should be. If we'd reacted that way, then the terrorists would have truly failed.

It's time we calm down and fight terror with antiterror. This does not mean that we simply roll over and accept terrorism. There are things our government can and should do to fight terrorism, most of them involving intelligence and investigation—and not focusing on specific plots.

But our job is to remain steadfast in the face of terror, to refuse to be terrorized. Our job is to not panic every time two Muslims stand together checking their watches. There are approximately 1 billion Muslims in the world, a large percentage of them not Arab, and about 320 million Arabs in the Middle East, the overwhelming majority of them not terrorists. Our job is to think critically and rationally, and to ignore the cacophony of other interests trying to use terrorism to advance political careers or increase a television show's viewership.

The surest defense against terrorism is to refuse to be terrorized. Our job is to recognize that terrorism is just one of the risks we face, and not a particularly common one at that. And our job is to fight those politicians who use fear as an excuse to take away our liberties and promote security theater that wastes money and doesn't make us any safer.

CHAPTER 4

Do Efforts to Enhance Homeland Security Threaten Civil Liberties?

Chapter Overview

David Cole

David Cole is a professor at Georgetown University Law Center, a volunteer attorney with the Center for Constitutional Rights, and legal affairs correspondent for The Nation.

The devastating terrorist attacks of September 11 have made all of us feel vulnerable in ways that we have never felt before, and many have argued that we may need to sacrifice some of our liberty in order to purchase greater security. But for the most part what we have done since September 11 is not to make the hard choice of choosing which of our liberties we are willing to forego, but rather to sacrifice their liberties—those of immigrants, and especially of Arab and Muslim immigrants—for the purported security of the rest of us. This double standard is an all too tempting way to strike the balance—it allows citizens to enjoy a sense of security without sacrificing their own liberty, but it is an illegitimate trade-off. It is likely to be counterproductive, as it will alienate the very communities that we most need to work with as we fight the war on terrorism. And in the end, it is a false trade-off, because what we do to immigrants today often creates a precedent for what we do to U.S. citizens tomorrow. . . .

So as we consider how our government should respond to the new threat of terrorism, we must avoid the easy way out of thinking that the sacrifices will affect only immigrants, or that the sacrifices will only be temporary. Rather, we must ask what sacrifices we are willing to make across the board and permanently. Only then will we have any chance of striking a proper balance between liberty and security.

David Cole, "Trading Liberty for Security after September 11," *Foreign Policy in Focus*, September, 2002. http://911digitalarchive.org.

History

This is hardly the first time that we have responded to fear by targeting immigrants and treating them as suspect because of their group identities rather than their individual conduct. In World War I, we imprisoned dissidents, most of them immigrants, merely for speaking out against the war. In World War II, we interned over 110,000 persons, again many of whom were immigrants, not because of individualized determinations that they posed a threat to national security or the war effort, but solely for their Japanese ancestry. And in the fight against Communism, which reached its height in the McCarthy era, we made it a crime even to be a member of the Communist Party, and passed the McCarran-Walter Act, which authorized the government to keep out and expel noncitizens who advocated Communism or belonged to the Communist Party.

While today's response may not yet match these historical overreactions, it is characterized by the same mistakes of principle—targeting vulnerable groups not for illegal conduct but for group identity or political affiliation, treating legitimate political activity as if it were a criminal offense, and bypassing measures designed to protect the innocent.

A Quaker immigrant who sent a book by Gandhi on the virtues of nonviolence to seek to persuade a group to disavow violence would also be deportable as a terrorist.

Guilt by Association and Political Spying

In October 2001, Congress passed the USA Patriot Act, under a threat from Attorney General John Ashcroft. Among other things, it imposes guilt by association on immigrants, a philosophy that the Supreme Court has condemned as "alien to the traditions of a free society and the First Amendment itself." Before the advent of the Patriot Act, aliens were deportable for engaging in or supporting terrorist activity. The Patriot Act makes them deportable for virtually any associational support that they offer to a "terrorist organization," irrespective of whether the alien's support has any connection to violence, much less terrorism. The Act defines "terrorist organization" as any group of two or more persons that uses or threatens to use a weapon against person or property, and therefore reaches any group that has ever been involved in a civil war or a crime of violence.

Under this provision, an alien who sent coloring books to a daycare center run by a designated organization would be deportable as a terrorist, even if she could show that the coloring books were used only by three-year-olds. Indeed, the law extends even to those who support a group in an effort to counter terrorism. Thus, a Quaker immigrant who sent a book by Gandhi on the virtues of nonviolence to seek to persuade a group to disavow violence would also be deportable as a terrorist.

Penalizing people for such conduct violates both the First and Fifth Amendments. All persons in the United States have a First Amendment right to associate with groups that have lawful and unlawful ends, so long as they do not further the group's illegal ends. And the Fifth Amendment dictates that "in our jurisprudence guilt is personal." Without some connection between the alien's support and terrorist activity, the Constitution is violated. . . .

Excluding people for their ideas is flatly contrary to the spirit of freedom for which the United States stands.

Ideological Exclusion

The Patriot Act also resurrects ideological exclusion, the practice of denying entry to aliens for pure speech. It excludes aliens who "endorse or espouse terrorist activity," or who "persuade others to support terrorist activity or a terrorist organization," or who belong to groups so advocating. Excluding people for their ideas is flatly contrary to the spirit of freedom for which the United States stands. For that reason, Congress in 1990 repealed all such grounds in the Immigration and Nationality Act. September 11 notwithstanding, surely we are a strong enough country, and our resolve against terrorism is powerful enough, to make such censorship unnecessary.

Detention Versus Due Process

Shortly after September 11, John Ashcroft announced that he would use every law on the books to catch "suspected terrorists" and lock them up. That preventive detention campaign has now involved the arrest of some 1,500–2,000 persons, yet not a single one has been charged with the crime under investigation or with terrorism. In fact, not only have none of the detainees been charged with a terrorist crime, but most have been affirmatively cleared by the FBI of any involvement in September 11, Al Qaeda, or any terrorist activity. The government's policy has been to find some pretext to arrest, and not to release or deport until the FBI has cleared the individual. In sum, we reversed the general rule—these persons, nearly all immigrants, were presumed guilty, arrested, and only then investigated and if cleared, released or deported. . . .

The administration also dramatically changed the rules that govern its authority to detain immigrants. Shortly after September 11, it gave the Immigration and Naturalization Service (INS) the authority to hold aliens without charges for an unspecified "reasonable" period in times of emergency. Many were held for weeks, and some for over a month, without any charges. The administration also changed the rules so that if an immigration judge orders an alien's release, the INS prosecutor can effectively overrule the judge and keep the alien locked up simply by filing an appeal.

The Patriot Act goes still further, giving the Attorney General unilateral authority to detain aliens on his own say-so, without any hearing or opportunity for the alien to respond to the charges. The Attorney General may detain any immigrant whom he certifies as a "suspected terrorist." The Patriot Act defines "suspected terrorist" so broadly that it includes virtually every immigrant who has been involved in a barroom brawl or domestic dispute, as well as aliens who have never committed an act of violence in their life, and whose only offense is to have provided humanitarian aid to an organization disfavored by the government. In some instances, the law authorizes the Attorney General to hold such persons indefinitely.

This provision violates the most basic elements of due process. It authorizes preventive detention of persons who pose no danger to the community or risk of flight. It authorizes detention without any notice or hearing. And it allows the INS to detain aliens indefinitely, even where they prevail in their removal proceedings by obtaining relief from removal. This is akin to detaining a prisoner after he has been pardoned. . . .

Military Justice

In November 2001, President Bush issued an unprecedented military order that authorizes dispensing with criminal trials and trying all aliens accused of terrorist acts or harboring terrorists in military tribunals. After much criticism, the military issued regulations that provided aliens in such proceedings with some protections. Yet even as amended, defendants in military tribunals will have no appeal to any independent court, and their conviction can be based on secret evidence that neither the defendant nor anyone outside the military would have an opportunity to review. In essence, the executive branch—and specifically the military—will be judge, jury, and executioner.

As yet, however, the military has not instituted a single trial. It has found it more convenient to hold individuals without trial, and has asserted the authority to hold persons indefinitely as "enemy combatants" incommunicado, without charges, and without access to lawyer. None of the hundreds of foreign citizens held on Guantanamo has had any kind of hearing at all.

That treatment, initially limited to noncitizens, has now been extended to U.S. citizens, in the cases of Yaser Hamdi and Jose Padilla. These two men, U.S. citizens, are held under essentially the same conditions as the foreign citizens on Guantanamo. The government has argued in legal proceedings that it has unlimited authority to hold them indefinitely, and that the courts have no role to play in questioning the executive's detention even of U.S. citizens. In short, even if Hamdi and Padilla are wholly innocent, they have no recourse.

The administration has grown increasingly bold in its assertions of authority, and has already begun to cross the citizen/noncitizen line that it initially relied upon to introduce many of its initiatives.

Operation Tips and National ID Cards

As the Hamdi and Padilla cases illustrate, the administration has grown increasingly bold in its assertions of authority, and has already begun to cross the citizen/noncitizen line that it initially relied upon to introduce many of its initiatives. Two recent examples are the proposals for a national identity card and for Operation TIPS, a program encouraging citizens to spy on one another. These proposals would affect all of us. We would all have to carry an official identity card, making it much easier for the government to trace our every step. And we would all have to worry about our neighbors or the delivery man spying on us and reporting any unusual behavior to the authorities. In practice, of course, Arabs, Muslims, and those who might be mistaken for Arabs or Muslims would bear the brunt of the harm, as they would disproportionately be the targets of identity stops and private snooping. But in another sense, we would all be affected, as the introduction of these programs would significantly change American life as we know it. Precisely for the latter reason, both proposals have received extensive criticism from across the political spectrum. At the insistence of Congressman Dick Armey, the House of Representatives' bill on the proposed Homeland Security department expressly bars development of a national identity card and implementation of the TIPS program. As these examples illustrate, the political process can much more reliably strike a balance between liberty and security when everyone has an interest on both sides of the line.

As a constitutional matter, due process and political freedoms of speech and association are not limited to citizens, but apply to all persons within the United States.

Why We Shouldn't Rely on Double Standards

The double standards outlined in this paper are wrong, unlikely to make us more secure, and likely to come back to haunt us all. First, as a constitutional matter, due process and political freedoms of speech and association are not limited to citizens, but apply to all persons within the United States. The Constitution does limit some rights to citizens—the right to vote and the right to run for certain federal offices—but those limitations only underscore that when the Constitution says "no person" shall be denied due process, it means no person. The Supreme Court has stated that the First and Fifth Amendments acknowledge no distinction between citizens and aliens living here. This understanding, moreover, is consistent with international human rights law, which guarantees to citizens and noncitizens alike the same due process and political speech and associational rights.

Second, these measures are unlikely to make us more secure. By penalizing even wholly nonviolent, and counterterrorist associational activity, we are likely to waste valuable resources tracking innocent political activity, drive other activity underground, encourage extremists, and make the communities that will inevitably be targeted by such measures far less likely to cooperate with law enforcement. And by conducting law enforcement in secret, and jettisoning procedures designed to protect the innocent and afford legitimacy to the outcome of trials, we will encourage people to fear the worst about our government. As Justice Louis Brandeis wrote nearly seventy-five years ago, the framers of our Constitution knew "that fear breeds repression; that repression breeds hate; and that hate menaces stable government." In other words, maintaining our freedoms is itself critical to maintaining our security.

George W. Bush's "War on Terror" Violates the Rule of Law

David Cole and Jules Lobel

David Cole is a legal affairs correspondent for The Nation, *a progressive political magazine, and a professor at Georgetown University Law Center. Jules Lobel is a professor at the University of Pittsburgh Law School.*

President George W. Bush is fond of reminding us that no terrorist attacks have occurred on domestic soil since 9/11. But has the Administration's "war on terror" actually made us safer? According to the July 2007 National Intelligence Estimate, Al Qaeda has fully reconstituted itself in Pakistan's northern border region. Terrorist attacks worldwide have grown dramatically in frequency and lethality since 2001. New terrorist groups, from Al Qaeda in Mesopotamia to the small groups of young men who bombed subways and buses in London and Madrid, have multiplied since 9/11. Meanwhile, despite the Bush Administration's boasts, the total number of people it has convicted of engaging in a terrorist act since 9/11 is one (Richard Reid, the shoe bomber)....

Few have asked whether "going on offense" actually works as a counterterrorism strategy. It doesn't. The Bush strategy has been a colossal failure, not only in terms of constitutional principle but in terms of national security. It turns out that in fighting terrorism, the best defense is not a good offense but a smarter defense.

David Cole and Jules Lobel, "Why We're Losing the War on Terror," *The Nation.com*, September 6, 2007. Reproduced by permission. www.thenation.com.

Preventive Anti-Terror Strategy Touches Many

"Going on offense," or the "paradigm of prevention," as then-Attorney General John Ashcroft dubbed it, has touched all of us. Some, like Canadian Maher Arar, have been rendered to third countries (in his case, Syria) to be interrogated by security services known for torture. Others have been subjected to months of virtually nonstop questioning, sexual abuse, waterboarding and injections with intravenous fluids until they urinate on themselves. Still others, like KindHearts, an American charity in Toledo, Ohio, have had their assets frozen under the USA Patriot Act and all their records seized without so much as a charge, much less a finding, of wrongdoing.

Thousands of Arab and Muslim immigrants have been singled out, essentially on the basis of their ethnicity or religion [by the Federal Bureau of Invesigation].

In the name of the "preventive paradigm," thousands of Arab and Muslim immigrants have been singled out, essentially on the basis of their ethnicity or religion, for special treatment, including mandatory registration, FBI [Federal Bureau of Investigation] interviews and preventive detention. Businesses have been served with more than 100,000 "national security letters," which permit the FBI to demand records on customers without a court order or individualized basis for suspicion. We have all been subjected to unprecedented secrecy about what elected officials are doing in our name while simultaneously suffering unprecedented official intrusion into our private lives by increased video surveillance, warrantless wiretapping and data-mining. Most tragically, more than 3,700 Americans and more than 70,000 Iraqi civilians have given their lives for the "preventive paradigm," which was used to justify going to war against a country that had not attacked us and posed no imminent threat of attack.

The Dangers of a Preventive Strategy

The preventive paradigm had its genesis on September 12, 2001. In [the 2002 book] *Bush at War*, Bob Woodward recounts a White House meeting in which FBI Director Robert Mueller advised that authorities must take care not to taint evidence in seeking 9/11 accomplices so that they could eventually be held accountable. Ashcroft immediately objected, saying, "The chief mission of US law enforcement . . . is to stop another attack and apprehend any accomplices. . . . If we can't bring them to trial, so be it." Ever since, the "war on terror" has been characterized by highly coercive, "forward-looking" pre-emptive measures—warrantless wiretapping, detention, coercive interrogation, even war—undertaken not on evidence of past or current wrongdoing but on speculation about future threats.

In isolation, neither the goal of preventing future attacks nor the tactic of using coercive measures is novel or troubling. All law enforcement seeks to prevent crime, and coercion is a necessary element of state power. However, when the end of prevention and the means of coercion are combined in the Administration's preventive paradigm, they produce a troubling form of anticipatory state violence—undertaken before wrongdoing has actually occurred and often without good evidence for believing that wrongdoing will ever occur.

The Bush strategy turns the law's traditional approach to state coercion on its head.

The Bush strategy turns the law's traditional approach to state coercion on its head. With narrow exceptions, the rule of law reserves invasions of privacy, detention, punishment and use of military force for those who have been shown—on the basis of sound evidence and fair procedures—to have committed or to be plotting some wrong. The police can tap phones or search homes, but only when there is probable cause to believe that a crime has been committed and that the search is likely to find evidence of the crime. People can be preventively detained pending trial, but only when there is both probable cause of past wrongdoing and concrete evidence that they pose a danger to the community or are likely to abscond if left at large. And under international law, nations may use military force unilaterally only in response to an objectively verifiable attack or threat of imminent attack.

These bedrock legal requirements are a hindrance to "going on offense." Accordingly, the Administration has asserted sweeping executive discretion, eschewed questions of guilt or innocence and substituted secrecy and speculation for accountability and verifiable fact. Where the rule of law demands fair and open procedures, the preventive paradigm employs truncated processes often conducted in secret, denying the accused a meaningful opportunity to respond. The need for pre-emptive action is said to justify secrecy and shortcuts, whatever the cost to innocents. Where the rule of law demands that people be held liable only for their own actions, the Administration has frequently employed guilt by association and ethnic profiling to target suspected future wrongdoers. And where the rule of law absolutely prohibits torture and disappearances, the preventive paradigm views these tactics as lesser evils to defuse the proverbial ticking time bomb.

The Administration has asserted sweeping executive discretion . . . and substituted secrecy and speculation for accountability and verifiable fact.

All other things being equal, preventing a terrorist act is, of course, preferable to responding after the fact—all the more so when the threats include weapons of mass destruction and our adversaries are difficult to detect, willing to kill themselves and seemingly unconstrained by any recognizable considerations of law, morality or human dignity. But there are plenty of preventive counterterrorism measures that conform to the rule of law, such as increased protections at borders and around vulnerable targets, institutional reforms designed to encourage better information sharing, even military force and military detention when employed in self-defense. The real problems arise when the state uses highly coercive measures—depriving people of their life, liberty or property, or going to war—based on speculation, without adhering to the laws long seen as critical to regulating and legitimizing such force.

An Ineffective Approach

Even if one were to accept as a moral or ethical matter the "ends justify the means" rationales advanced for the preventive paradigm, the paradigm fails its own test: There is little or no evidence that the Administration's coercive pre-emptive measures have made us safer, and substantial evidence that they have in fact exacerbated the dangers we face. Consider the costliest example: the war in Iraq. Precisely because the preventive doctrine turns on speculation about non-imminent events, it permitted the Administration to turn its focus from Al Qaeda, the organization that attacked us on 9/11, to Iraq, a nation that did not. The Iraq War has by virtually all accounts made the United States, the Iraqi people, many of our allies and for that matter much of the world more vulnerable to terrorists. By targeting Iraq, the Bush Administration not only siphoned off much-needed resources from the struggle against Al Qaeda but also created a golden opportunity for Al Qaeda to inspire and recruit others to attack US and allied targets. And our invasion of Iraq has turned it into the world's premier terrorist training ground.

The preventive paradigm has been no more effective in other aspects of the "war on terror." According to US figures, international terrorist attacks increased by 300 percent between 2003 and 2004. In 2005 alone, there were 360 suicide bombings, resulting in 3,000 deaths, compared with an annual average of about ninety such attacks over the five preceding years. That hardly constitutes progress.

But what about the fact that, other than the anthrax mailings in 2001, there has not been another terrorist attack in the United States since 9/11? The real question, of course, is whether the Administration's coercive preventive measures can be credited for that. There were eight years between the first and second attacks on the World Trade Center. And when one looks at what the preventive paradigm has come up with in terms of concrete results, it's an astonishingly thin file. At Guantánamo [a US detention center in Cuba], for example, once said to house "the worst of the worst," the Pentagon's Combatant Status Review Tribunals' own findings categorized only 8 percent of some 500 detainees held there in 2006 as fighters for Al Qaeda or the Taliban. More than half of the 775 Guantánamo detainees have now been released, suggesting that they may not have been "the worst of the worst" after all.

As for terror cells at home, the FBI admitted in February 2005 that it had yet to identify a single Al Qaeda sleeper cell in the entire United States. And it hasn't found any since— unless you count the Florida group arrested in 2006, whose principal step toward an alleged plot to blow up the Sears Tower was to order combat boots and whose only Al Qaeda "connection" was to a federal informant pretending to be Al Qaeda.

The Justice Department claims on its website www.lifeandliberty.gov to have charged more than 400 people in "terrorism-related" cases, but its own Inspector General has criticized those figures as inflated. The vast majority of the cases involved not terrorism but minor nonviolent offenses such as immigration fraud, credit-card fraud or lying to an FBI agent. The *New York Times* and the *Washington Post* found that only thirty-nine of the convictions were for a terrorism crime. And virtually all of those were for "material support" to groups labeled terrorist, a crime that requires no proof that the defendant ever intended to further a terrorist act. While prosecutors have obtained a handful of convictions for conspiracy to engage in terrorism, several of those convictions rest on extremely broad statutes that don't require proof of any specific plan or act, or on questionable entrapment tactics by government informants. Many of the Administration's most highly touted "terrorism" cases have disintegrated after the Justice Department's initial self-congratulatory press conference announcing the indictment. . . .

Many of the Administration's most highly touted "terror-ism" cases have disintegrated after the Justice Department's initial self-congratulatory press conference.

Less Security

If the Bush strategy were merely ineffectual, that would be bad enough. But it's worse than that; the President's policy has actually made us significantly less secure. While the Administration has concentrated on swaggeringly aggressive coercive initiatives of dubious effect, it has neglected less dramatic but more effective preventive initiatives. In December 2005 the bipartisan 9/11 Commission gave the Administration failing or near-failing grades on many of the most basic domestic security measures, including assessing critical infrastructure vulnerabilities, securing weapons of mass destruction, screening airline passengers and cargo, sharing information between law enforcement and intelligence agencies, insuring that first responders have adequate communications and supporting secular education in Muslim countries. We spend more in a day in Iraq than we do annually on some of the most important defensive initiatives here at home.

The preventive paradigm has also made it more difficult to bring terrorists to justice, just as FBI Director Mueller warned on September 12 [2007]. When the Administration chooses to disappear suspects into secret prisons and use waterboarding to encourage them to talk, it forfeits any possibility of bringing the suspects to justice for their alleged crimes, because evidence obtained coercively at a "black site" would never be admissible in a fair and legitimate trial. That's the real reason no one has yet been brought to trial at Guantánamo. There is debate about whether torture ever results in reliable intelligence—but there can be no debate that it radically curtails the government's ability to bring a terrorist to justice.

Assuming that the principal terrorist threat still comes from Al Qaeda or, more broadly, a violence-prone fundamentalist strain of Islam, and that the "enemies" in this struggle are a relatively small number of Arab and Muslim men, it is all the more critical that we develop close, positive ties with Arab and Muslim communities here and abroad. By alienating those whose help we need most, the preventive paradigm has had exactly the opposite effect. At the same time, we have given Al Qaeda the best propaganda it could ever have hoped for. Then-Defense Secretary Donald Rumsfeld identified the critical question in an October 2003 internal Pentagon memo: "Are we capturing, killing or deterring and dissuading more terrorists every day than the madrassas and the radical clerics are recruiting, training and deploying against us?" While there is no precise metric for answering Rumsfeld's question, there can be little doubt that our preventive tactics have been a boon to terrorist recruitment throughout the world.

More broadly still, our actions have radically undermined our standing in the world. The damage to US prestige was perhaps most dramatically revealed when, after the report of CIA [Central Intelligence Agency] black sites [secret interrogation locations] surfaced in November 2005, Russia, among several other countries, promptly issued a press release claiming that it had nothing to do with the sites. When Russia feels the need to distance itself from the United States out of concern that its human rights image might be tarnished by association, we have fallen far. In short, we have gone from being the object of the world's sympathy immediately after 9/11 to being the country most likely to be hated. Anti-Americanism is at an all-time high. In some countries, Osama bin Laden has a higher approval rating than the United States. And much of the anti-Americanism is tied to the perception that the United States has pursued its "war on terror" in an arrogant, unilateral fashion, defying the very values we once championed.

The Bush Administration just doesn't get it. Its National Defense Strategy, published by the Pentagon, warns that "our strength as a nation state will continue to be challenged by those who employ a strategy of the weak using international fora, judicial processes, and terrorism." The proposition that judicial processes and international accountability—the very essence of the rule of law—are to be dismissed as a strategy of the weak, aligned with terrorism itself, makes clear that the Administration has come to view the rule of law as an obstacle, not an asset, in its effort to protect us from terrorist attack. Our long-term security turns not on "going on offense" by locking up thousands of "suspected terrorists" who turn out to have no connection to terrorism; nor on forcing suspects to bark like dogs, urinate and defecate on themselves, and endure sexual humiliation; nor on attacking countries that have not threatened to attack us. Security rests not on exceptionalism and double standards but on a commitment to fairness, justice and the rule of law. The rule of law in no way precludes a state from defending itself from terrorists but requires that it do so within constraints. And properly understood, those constraints are assets, not obstacles. Aharon Barak, who recently retired as president of Israel's Supreme Court, said it best in a case forbidding the use of "moderate physical pressure" in interrogating Palestinian terror suspects: "A democracy must sometimes fight terror with one hand tied behind its back. Even so, a democracy has the upper hand. The rule of law and the liberty of an individual constitute important components in its understanding of security. At the end of the day, they strengthen its spirit and this strength allows it to overcome its difficulties."

The preventive paradigm has compromised our spirit, strengthened our enemies and left us less free and less safe. If we are ready to learn from our mistakes, however, there is a better way to defend ourselves—through, rather than despite, a recommitment to the rule of law.

The Revised Patriot Act Is Unconstitutional

Ryan Singel

Ryan Singel is a San Francisco-based journalist.

A U.S. District Court struck down a key provision of the Patriot Act as unconstitutional Thursday, marking the second time that a provision which allows anti-terrorism investigators to write their own subpoenas for phone and internet records and require the recipients to never speak of them violated the First Amendment.

The ruling strikes yet another blow at the FBI's use of National Security Letters.

The ruling strikes yet another blow at the FBI's [Federal Bureau of Investigation] use of National Security Letters [NSLs], which were used to issue 143,074 requests for phone and internet records from 2003 to 2005, and as a recent Inspector General report showed, the widespread use led to abuses and sloppiness. Early this year, a damning report by the Justice Department's Inspector General found that the FBI used NSLs in violation of applicable NSL statutes, Attorney General guidelines and internal FBI policies. The FBI, along with the Inspector General, are now criminally investigating an office that sent more than 700 emergency letters, with false statements in them, to phone companies.

The ACLU [American Civil Liberties Union] sued on behalf of an anonymous internet service provider [ISP], which was served an NSL about one of the websites it hosted. The ISP contested the order, which the FBI subsequently dropped,

Ryan Singel, "Court Strikes Down Key Patriot Act Power Again," *Wired.com*, September 6, 2007. Copyright © 2008 Conde Nast Publications. All rights reserved. Originally published in Wired.com. Reprinted with permission. http://blog.wired.com.

but the ISP remains unable to even acknowledge that it got a request, and the company's president said he's been forced to lie to his friends and girlfriend about it.

Judge Victor Marrero of the Southern District of New York ruled that the gag order and the strict rules about how to contest them amounted to prior restraint on speech and allowed the FBI to pick and choose which persons would be gagged, based on whether the feds believed the target might speak critically of the government. Judge Marrero found, in a 106 page opinion, that the gag order provisions couldn't be struck down without affecting the rest of the statute so he found that the entire NSL provision was unconstitutional. He also stuck down a provision that prescribed the standards courts should use in judging the FBI's arguments for keeping gag orders. Marrero wrote that Congress had overstepped its bounds in setting out those standards.

The judge also made it clear that the scope of the FBI's powers, which were not challenged by the ACLU, concerned the court:

> But as powerful and valuable it may be as a means of surveillance and as crucial the purpose it serves, the NSL nevertheless poses profound concerns to our society, not the least of which, as reported by the OIG [Office of the Inspector General], is the potential for abuse of its employment. Through the use of NSLs, the government can unmask the identity of internet users engaged in anonymous speech in online discussions. It can obtain an itemized list of all the emails sent and received by the target of the NSL, and it can then seek information on individuals communicating with that person. It may be even be able to discover the websites an individual has visited and queries submitted to search engines.

This is the second time the NSL statute has been struck down in this case. After the last decision, the Administration loosened the gag order provision, which in the original Patriot

Act, could not be contested and lasted in perpetuity. In the Patriot Act Re-Authorization, the FBI had the option to add gag orders to NSLs and recipients could choose to fight them in court once a year. But the law established rules saying that courts had to give great deference to the FBI's national security arguments.

Judge Marrero decided those changes did not go far enough:

> In granting the FBI authority to certify that an NSL recipient cannot disclose to any person information about receipt of the NSL, and in including this prescription in the actual NSL letter issued, the amended [statute] "authorizes suppression of speech in advance of its expression."

The order is being stayed for 90 days to give the government time to appeal the order or get Congress to rewrite the gag rules yet again.

The Government's Data-Mining Program Is an Unprecedented Assault on Privacy

Shane Harris and Tim Naftali

Shane Harris is a staff correspondent for National Journal, *a magazine about national politics. Tim Naftali is the director of the Presidential Recordings Program at the University of Virginia's Miller Center of Public Affairs.*

Fifty years ago, officers from the Signal Security Agency, the predecessor to the National Security Agency [NSA], visited an executive from International Telephone and Telegraph [ITT] and asked for copies of all foreign government cables carried by the company. The request was a direct violation of a 1934 law that banned the interception of domestic communications, but Attorney General Tom Clark backed it. Initially reluctant, ITT relented when told that its competitor, Western Union, had already agreed to supply this information. As James Bamford relates in his book *The Puzzle Palace*, the government told ITT it "would not desire to be the only noncooperative company on the project." Codenamed Shamrock, the effort to collect cables sent through U.S.-controlled telegraph lines ultimately involved all the American telecom giants of the era, captured private as well as government cables, and lasted nearly 30 years. Like other illegal Cold War domestic snooping programs—such as the FBI's [Federal Bureau of Investigation] wiretaps without warrants and the CIA's [Central Intelligence Agency] mail-opening operations—it collapsed under the weight of public reaction to the abuses of executive power revealed by Vietnam and Watergate.

Shane Harris and Tim Naftali, "Tinker, Tailor, Minor, Spy: Why the NSA's Snooping Is Unprecedented in Scale and Scope," *Slate.com*, January 3, 2006. Distributed by United Feature Syndicate, Inc. http://www.slate.com.

Current NSA Spying

Today's generation of telecom leaders is similarly involved in the current controversy over spying by the NSA. The *New York Times* reported in December [2005] that since 9/11, leading telecommunications companies "have been storing information on calling patterns and giving it to the federal government to aid in tracking possible terrorists." Citing current and former government and corporate officials, the *Times* reported that the companies have granted the NSA access to their all-important switches, the hubs through which colossal volumes of voice calls and data transmissions move every second. A former telecom executive told us that efforts to obtain call details go back to early 2001, predating the 9/11 attacks and the president's now celebrated secret executive order. The source, who asked not to be identified so as not to out his former company, reports that the NSA approached U.S. carriers and asked for their cooperation in a "data-mining" operation, which might eventually cull "millions" of individual calls and e-mails.

Like the pressure applied to ITT a half-century ago, our source says the government was insistent, arguing that his competitors had already shown their patriotism by signing on. The NSA would not comment on the issue, saying that, "We do not discuss details of actual or alleged operational issues."

The NSA [National Security Agency is conducting] a "data-mining" operation, which might eventually cull "millions" of individual calls and e-mails.

A New Method of Spying

The magnitude of the current collection effort is unprecedented and indeed marks a shift in how the NSA spies in the United States. The current program seems to involve a remarkable level of cooperation with private companies and extraordinarily expansive data-mining of questionable legality. Before Bush authorized the NSA to expand its domestic snooping program after 9/11 in the secret executive order, the agency had to stay clear of the "protected communications" of American citizens or resident aliens unless supplied by a judge with a warrant. The program President Bush authorized reportedly allows the NSA to mine huge sets of domestic data for suspicious patterns, regardless of whether the source of the data is an American citizen or resident. The NSA needs the help of private companies to do this because commercial broadband now carries so many communications. In an earlier age, the NSA could pick up the bulk of what it needed by tapping into satellite or microwave transmissions. "Now," as the agency noted in a transition document prepared for the incoming Bush administration in December 2000, "communications are mostly digital, carry billions of bits of data, and contain voice, data and multimedia. They are dynamically routed, globally networked and pass over traditional communications means such as microwave or satellite less and less."

The agency used to search the transmissions it monitors for key words, such as names and phone numbers, which are supplied by other intelligence agencies that want to track certain individuals. But now the NSA appears to be vacuuming up all data, generally without a particular phone line, name, or e-mail address as a target. Reportedly, the agency is analyzing the length of a call, the time it was placed, and the origin and destination of electronic transmissions. Those details would be crucial in mining the data for patterns—according to the officials the *Times* cited, the goal of the NSA's eavesdropping system.

Pattern-based searches are most useful when run against huge sets of data. Many calls and messages must be analyzed to determine which ones are benign and which deserve more attention. With large data sets, pattern-based searching can create more nuanced pictures of the connections among people, places, and messages. Deputy Director of National Intelligence Michael Hayden, who until this year was the NSA director, recently hinted that the NSA's eavesdropping program is not just looking for transmissions from specific individuals. It has a "subtly softer trigger" that initiates monitoring without exactly knowing in advance what specific transmissions to look for. Presumably, this trigger is a suspicious pattern. But officials have not actually described any triggers, raising the question of whether the NSA has been authorized to go on such fishing expeditions.

A Lack of Safeguards

The government experimented with large-scale pattern-based searches under the auspices of the Defense Department's Total Information Awareness [TIA] program in 2002. The aim was to sift though government intelligence data, and also privately held information, for telltale signs of the planning of a terrorist attack. TIA was ridiculed as Orwellian [a reference to George Orwell's book *1984*]. But at least the program tried to create new technologies to protect personal information. Adm. John Poindexter, TIA's creator, believed in the potential intelligence benefits of data-mining broadband communications, but he was also well aware of the potential for excess. "We need a much more systematic approach" to data-mining and privacy protection, Poindexter said at a 2002 conference in Anaheim, Calif., sponsored by the Defense Advanced Research Projects Agency. Poindexter envisioned a "privacy appliance," a device that would strip any identifiers from the information—such as names or addresses—so that government miners could see only patterns. Then if there was reason to believe that the information belonged to a group that was planning an attack, the government could seek a warrant and disable the privacy control for that specific data. TIA funded research on a privacy appliance at the Palo Alto Research Center, a subsidiary of Xerox Corp. "The idea is that this device, cryptographically protected to prevent tampering, would ensure that no one could abuse private information without an immutable digital record of their misdeeds," according to a 2003 government report to Congress about TIA. "The details of the operation of the appliance would be available to the public."

The magnitude of the current collection effort is unprecedented and indeed marks a shift in how the NSA [National Security Agency] spies in the United States.

The NSA's domestic eavesdropping program, however, appears to have none of these safeguards. When Congress killed TIA's funding in 2003, it effectively ended research into privacy-protection technology. According to former officials associated with TIA, after the program was canceled, elements of it were transferred into the classified intelligence budget. But these did not include research on privacy protection.

In January, Congress plans to hold hearings into the legality of the Bush administration's eavesdropping program. Lawmakers will want to know why, if the NSA cannot do its job while remaining within the legal bounds established in the 1970s, the Bush administration did not address that problem in the context of the Patriot Act. Congress might also ask why in the rush to begin data-mining, the NSA has abandoned the privacy controls planned for the TIA. As Adm. Poindexter himself noted in his resignation letter from the program in 2003, "it would be no good to solve the security problem and give up the privacy and civil liberties that make our country great."

The Real ID Act Will Clearly Invade Americans' Privacy

Michael Hampton

Michael Hampton is editor and publisher of Homeland Stupidity, *a blog about government blunders and incompetence.*

The Real ID Act of 2005, which mandates that states conform their driver's licenses and identification cards to a common standard defined by the Department of Homeland Security and that states put personal information into a central database, is being sold as a secure document which will protect us all from terrorism, illegal immigration and identity theft. But it will do no such thing.

Bush Administration Support for Real ID

Secretary of Homeland Security Michael Chertoff defended Real ID . . . saying that the initiative would help prevent identity theft and illegal immigration and promote privacy. "I think this is an example where security and privacy go hand-in-hand," he said Thursday. "It is a win-win for both if we are disciplined and intelligent about the way we analyze the risks."

First, there's illegal immigration and identity theft. Someone gets hold of your personal information and gets a job, or a bank account, or a credit card, with your name and Social Security number. "For every single person whose identity was stolen by someone who forged their name and their Social Security number on a driver's license, or on an identification document, ask that person, do you feel your privacy is better protected if someone can walk around with phony documents, with your name and your number?" he said. "Or is your privacy better protected if you have the confidence that

Michael Hampton, "Chertoff: Real ID Not 'Invasion of Privacy,'" *Homeland Stupidity*, December 17, 2006. Reproduced by permission. www.homelandstupidity.us.

the identification relied upon is, in fact, secure and reliable, and uniquely tied to a single individual?"

[Real ID] won't stop most types of identity theft at all, since the ID itself isn't required, only the information.

False Arguments

But Real ID won't stop phony documents. It may make them harder to get, but there are plenty of corrupt DMV [Department of Motor Vehicles] employees ready and willing to provide real identification to anyone who pays a hefty enough bribe. Indeed, it won't stop most types of identity theft at all, since the ID itself isn't required, only the information.

And it won't stop illegal immigration. I suspect Chertoff knows this. He's previously admitted that he knows why people come here. "We all know that the primary economic engine that draws in illegal migration is work," he said. But one can make up a phony name and number on the spot and work. Or a person can work under the table. The Real ID won't stop any of this.

Finally, there's terrorism. The 9/11 Commission recommended that "Secure identification should begin in the United States. The federal government should set standards for the issuance of birth certificates and sources of identification, such as drivers licenses." The justification for this? "At many entry points to vulnerable facilities, including gates for boarding aircraft, sources of identification are the last opportunity to ensure that people are who they say they are and to check whether they are terrorists."

Real ID does precious little to help authorities determine who might or might not be a threat. The 9/11 hijackers, the 9/11 Commission was forced to admit, just walked right into local DMV offices and got driver's licenses in their own names! There's no reason to think future terrorists could not also do this under Real ID.

So what exactly is the point to Real ID? Who is being made secure, and why does Chertoff think it's a "win-win" for privacy?

The central databases required by Real ID ... [will] be maintained ... by a private company ..., [letting] the federal government bypass Privacy Act protections.

The Real Purpose for Real ID

As we now know, the central databases required by Real ID won't be maintained by the federal government, but by a private company. This lets the federal government bypass Privacy Act protections when it wants access to that data. It also reduces the protection you have against bad information getting into the database. It would have been easy enough for the government to track you with the data in a government database, but with it in a commercial database, it's even easier. "Is this somehow an invasion of privacy?" Chertoff asks. No reasonable person could possibly answer "no."

Then there's the money. Real ID is an $11 billion unfunded mandate that states must comply with or risk losing federal highway funding. States can't absorb all the costs associated with compliance, so Real ID compliant driver's license costs could exceed $100 each.

It's also worth mentioning that many people consider Real ID to be the "Mark of the Beast," without which people won't be able to participate in ordinary commerce, and with which people won't be allowed to enter the Kingdom of Heaven. Without a Real ID compliant identification card, people won't be allowed to enter airports or federal buildings, receive government services, and quite possibly be barred from doing business with banks and other financial institutions.

The only purpose behind an identification card is to allow the government to require you to show it to them. Is that the sort of country we want to be? Didn't we do battle with a country just like that 60 years ago? How far America has fallen.

The 2007 Protect America Act Poses a Serious Civil Liberties Threat

John W. Dean

John W. Dean, a former counsel to the president, is now an author and a columnist at FindLaw, *a legal Web site.*

Congressional Democrats are getting a lot of well-earned heat from rank-and-file members of their party, not to mention editorial writers and bloggers, for their lack of spine in refusing to reject the [George W.] Bush/[Dick] Cheney Administration's sweeping amendments to the Foreign Intelligence Surveillance Act (FISA). Just before Congress departed for its August [2007] recess, the Administration jammed through in five days—from start to finish—the dubiously titled Protect America Act (PAA) of 2007, over the protest of the Democratic leadership. The only thing good about the PAA is that it is temporary—with a six month expiration date (although surveillance programs authorized under it can operate for up to one year.)

On her *Democracy NOW* daily program, Amy Goodman ... interviewed *Salon.com*'s law blogger, Glenn Greenwald, and the president of the National Lawyers Guild, Marjorie Cohn, about the PAA. The interview nicely sets forth what happened and its broad implications. Simply stated, Bush threatened to make a political issue of any effort by Congressional Democrats to protect the civil liberties of Americans. Bush surely succeeded beyond his most fervent hope in his intimidation of sixteen Democratic members in the Senate and forty-one Democratic members in the House, earning these members a place on "the roll of shame" in the blogosphere.

John W. Dean, "The So-Called Protect America Act: Why Its Sweeping Amendments to the Foreign Intelligence Surveillance Act Pose Not Only a Civil Liberties Threat, But a Greater Danger as Well," *FindLaw*, August 10, 2007. Reproduced by permission. http://writ.news.findlaw.com.

A Threat Greater than That to Civil Liberties: Executive Aggrandizement

The Washington Post, the *New York Times*, and politically diverse organizations ranging from the John Birch Society and the Cato Institute to the American Civil Liberties Union all agree that the PAA is a serious mistake, and a threat to the civil liberties of Americans. They point out that the law ignores the Fourth Amendment while, at the same time, hiding its actual operations in national security secrecy. Indeed, Congress was not even certain about the full extent of what it has authorized because President Bush and Vice-President Cheney refused to reveal it.

It is not likely that law-abiding Americans will even know that the U.S. Government ... [is] listening in on their calls to and from foreign countries, or similarly scanning emails.

It is not likely that law-abiding Americans will even know that the U.S. Government's intelligence gathering operations are listening in on their calls to and from foreign countries, or similarly scanning emails. For this reason, it is not to be expected that many Americans will care about what the Democratic Congress has given a Republican president who has proven himself insensitive to anyone's privacy other than his own.

There is, however, a threat in this new law even greater than its robbing Americans of their communications privacy, which commentators and critics have virtually ignored. This law is another bold and blatant move by Bush to enhance the powers of the Executive branch at the expense of its constitutional co-equals.

Congress was willing to give Bush the amendments to FISA that would make this law effective under current technology. The 1978 law did not account for the fact that modern digital communications between people outside the United States often is routed through the United States, yet the FISA Court said surveillance of such routed communications required a warrant. Nevertheless, Bush rejected the legislation proposed by the Democrats because it also contained checks on the use of surveillance powers.

This, of course, is consistent with Bush and Cheney's general drive to weaken or eliminate all checks and balances constraining the Executive. This drive was evidenced by countless laws enacted by the Republican-controlled Congresses during the first six years of the Administration, and in countless signing statements added by the President interpreting away any constraints on the Executive. Thus, when even the GOP [Grand Old Party, referring to the Republican Party] Congresses required presidential compliance and reporting, they were thwarted.

The most stunning aspect of the Democrats' capitulation is their abandoning of their institutional responsibility to hold the president accountable. The Protect America Act utterly fails to maintain any real check on the president's power to undertake electronic surveillance of literally millions of Americans. This is an invitation to abuse, especially for a president like the current incumbent.

Fixing the Protect America Act

Though it is quite certain abuses of the surveillance powers under the Protect America Act will occur, they have not yet occurred. The failure to provide a check on such potential abuses, however, has already occurred. It represents the greatest failing of the Democratic Congress in acceding to the demands of Bush and Cheney. It is this failure that should be a paramount concern of the Congress when it next addresses this temporary law.

Speaker of the House Nancy Pelosi sent a letter to the chairmen of the House Judiciary Committee and the House

Intelligence Committee, requesting they develop legislation "addressing the many deficiencies" of the temporary law as soon as Congress returns from its recess.

Even though the White House got everything it demanded from Congress, it is requesting even more. When signing the Protect America Act, Bush said, "When Congress returns in September, the Intelligence Committees and leaders in both parties will need to complete work on the comprehensive reforms requested by Director of National Intelligence Mike McConnell, including the important issues of providing meaningful liability protection to those who are alleged to have assisted our Nation following the attacks of September 11, 2001."

No Congress should trust any president with unbridled powers of surveillance over Americans.

Bush also wants legislative immunity for the American companies, and government officials (including himself), to protect them from criminal prosecution for violating the criminal provision of FISA. As readers will recall, before Congress caved and gave Bush power to conduct this surveillance, he—and telecommunication companies—simply opted to do so illegally. Now, Bush will claim, with some justification, that because Congress has now made legal actions that were previously illegal, it should retroactively clear up this nasty problem facing all those who broke the law at his command.

If the Democrats fail to stand up to the bullying of this weak president, and ignore his demands for more unaccountability, they might as well start looking for another line of work. Not only are their fellow rank and file Democrats going to turn on them in 2008, but the overwhelming numbers of independents who assisted them in regaining power are going to desert them in droves. At bottom, Democrats truly only need to add one fix to this dangerous law: meaningful accountability. They must do so, or face the consequences.

No one wants to deny the intelligence community all the tools it needs. But regardless of who sits in the Oval Office, no Congress should trust any president with unbridled powers of surveillance over Americans. It is not the way our system is supposed to work.

The Patriot Act Has Not Abused Civil Liberties

Paul Rosenzweig

Paul Rosenzweig is a senior legal research fellow in the Center for Legal and Judicial Studies at The Heritage Foundation, a public policy think tank.

And so John Ashcroft's tenure as Attorney General of the United States has come to an end. [Ashcroft resigned February 3, 2005]. His opponents will rejoice, his supporters despair. Assuredly, he will be remembered, more so than most other Attorneys General are. But when the history is written, when his accomplishments are assessed not by partisans of the immediate here and now but by more dispassionate and objective analysts of the future, how will John Ashcroft be remembered? What will be his legacy?

Save for one event, Ashcroft's tenure would have been remembered as a comparatively successful one for a law-and-order Attorney General. Violent crimes have been reduced to their lowest level in 30 years. Drug-trafficking prosecutions against major narcotics dealers are up, and the Department of Justice's task force on corporate crime has aggressively pursued boardroom fraudsters. This is a solid record to be proud of, to be sure, but it is nothing earth-shattering.

[Former Attorney General John] Ashcroft will be remembered as the first Attorney General to confront terrorism seriously.

That one other event, however, changes the entire perspective: Because of September 11, Ashcroft will be remembered as

Paul Rosenzweig, "The Ashcroft Legacy: Liberty and Security," *The Heritage Foundation*, Webmemo #607, November 10, 2004. Reproduced by permission. www.heritage.org.

the first Attorney General to confront terrorism seriously. And though his critics have not been kind and his efforts have not been completely free of missteps, when history looks back on Ashcroft's efforts it will treat him quite well.

Ashcroft's Anti-Terror Successes

Consider the obvious first—more than three years have passed since September 11, and there have not been any attacks on the United States. This is not for lack of desire on the part of al-Qaeda. Of course, domestic law enforcement efforts don't tell the whole story of that effort—no doubt our offensive efforts in Afghanistan also played a significant role. But on the domestic front, through efforts led by Attorney General Ashcroft, we have broken up terrorist sleeper cells all across the country, and we have frozen more than $140 million in terrorist assets. These are not idle statistics; they are real threats disrupted.

The case of Mohammad Junneh Barbar illustrates the point. As recently as February 2004, Barbar was in Waziristan, the unruly province in northern Pakistan where the remnants of al-Qaeda are thought to lurk. Barbar, a United States citizen, recently admitted to a plan to ship military equipment to al-Qaeda in Waziristan. In another part of his plot, he bought bomb-making materials and operated a jihadi camp with the intent to conduct a bombing campaign. Rigorous investigation and law enforcement uncovered Barbar's activities and thwarted his plans, and he now sits in a federal prison, having been convicted of providing material support to terrorists.

But even more significant than the legal efforts initiated by Attorney General Ashcroft is the beginning of the long and difficult task of changing the culture of non-cooperation between the FBI [Federal Bureau of Investigation] and CIA [Central Inteligence Agency]. As any experienced staff member in either agency will tell you, before September 11 [2001] the two agencies were barely on speaking terms. And culture like that is hard to change—it will take a long time. But under Attorney General Ashcroft's leadership, with strong assistance from FBI Director Robert Mueller, the FBI has done its part to begin to shift that culture. We see greater cooperation and more information sharing today than ever in the past. And that change, so seemingly process oriented and insignificant, is an important building block in creating the structures and systems that will see us through a protracted conflict with radical terrorists.

Civil Liberties Protections

Critics will say that Ashcroft's successes pale beside his failures—in the aftermath of his resignation they will no doubt try to paint him as insensitive to civil liberties and uncaring about legal niceties. They are wrong.

Most of the tales of abuse and misuse [regarding the Patriot Act] are based on mistaken information.

Consider one example, the Patriot Act. As the Heritage Foundation report "A Patriot Act Reader" details, most of the tales of abuse and misuse are based on mistaken information. Even Russ Feingold, the only Senator to vote against the Patriot Act, says that he is in favor of 90 percent of it. And potential critics as diverse as the Inspector General for the Department of Justice and Senators Joseph Biden (D-DE) and Diane Feinstein (D-CA) say that they can't find any real evidence of abuse. In fact, with respect to one often-criticized provision of the Patriot Act (the so-called "Sneak and Peek" provision), Senator Feinstein has said that the law is actually an *improvement* for civil liberties and that it offers *more* protection against unlawful intrusions by law enforcement than did the pre-Patriot Act law.

And what of other alleged abuses? Again, they are mostly the stuff of legend. Take one notorious example—the arrest of more than 700 immigrants of Arab descent in New York in the immediate aftermath of the September 11 attacks. As the DOJ [Department of Justice] Inspector General has explained, the systems used by the FBI and INS [Immigration and Naturalization Service] for arresting and detaining immigrants broke down during that hectic period—in large part because they were never designed for a tragedy on such a scale. Far too many immigrants were held for too long and were not told why they had been detained. There were even instances of physical abuse by Bureau of Prison officers that are completely inexcusable. America can, and should, do better.

But what critics neglect is that during Attorney General Ashcroft's time in office it has. The Inspector General's report listed dozens of recommendations for change—recommendations and criticism that made front-page news across the country. The Inspector General's subsequent report, made 12 months later, says that the Department and the INS have undertaken the difficult work of putting into place new procedures that, should another catastrophic attack occur, will prevent a repetition of those procedural errors. This second report did not make the headlines, though it is arguably the more important of the two.

No First Amendment liberties have been curtailed, no dissent or criticism suppressed.

The Right Path

And that, in the end, captures what is perhaps John Ashcroft's greatest success. He has begun to put in place processes and systems of law that will stand us in good stead for the future. After all, any new system of laws and law enforcement procedures that we develop and implement must be designed to be tolerable over the long term. The war against terrorism, like the Cold War, is one with no immediately foreseeable end. Thus, excessive intrusions of civil rights cannot be justified as merely emergency measures that will lapse upon the termination of hostilities. Instead, policymakers must be restrained because Americans could have to live with the war on terror and the policies with which we wage it for many years.

By that measure, John Ashcroft's tenure has been a success. Many of the steps taken to combat terror had already been used to combat organized crime. And there is little evidence of any real abuse. No First Amendment liberties have been curtailed, no dissent or criticism suppressed. While Thomas Jefferson was right that we must be cautious and guard against governmental excess, John Locke, the seventeenth-century philosopher who greatly influenced the Founding Fathers, was equally right when he wrote, "In all states of created beings, capable of laws, where there is no law there is no freedom. For liberty is to be free from the restraint and violence from others; which cannot be where there is no law; and is not, as we are told, a liberty for every man to do what he lists." Thus, the government has two obligations: to protect civil safety and security against violence and to preserve civil liberty. Or as [intelligence expert] Thomas Powers has put it, "In a liberal republic, liberty presupposes security; the point of security is liberty."

John Ashcroft's success is in recognizing that achieving these goals is not a zero-sum game. We can achieve both— liberty and security—to an appreciable degree. Indeed, if there is any lesson to be learned from the Cold War, it is that we must pursue both, for otherwise we risk becoming like those whom we oppose. Ashcroft's tenure will be remembered for having set us on that right path.

Data Mining Could Help Catch Terrorists

Hiawatha Bray

Hiawatha Bray is a technology reporter for the Boston Globe.

Did US military spies finger Mohammed Atta as an Al Qaeda terrorist a year before the Sept. 11 attacks? A US congressman says yes; leaders of the bipartisan 9/11 investigating commission say no. But the controversy should remind us of one indisputable fact: A technology that may have helped spot Atta and other terrorists is being suppressed by Congress, for no particularly good reason. That technology is "data mining," the use of sophisticated software and powerful computers to spot patterns of activity hidden in vast amounts of apparently random data. It's used routinely by businesses seeking new ways to empty our wallets.

When you swipe one of those discount cards at the supermarket, you're letting the retailer make a record of everything you buy. Thus the store develops a profile of its customers' tastes and buying habits. Mining this data can reveal patterns that would otherwise go unnoticed. For instance, purchases of bottled water may increase whenever there's a sale on sirloin steak. Data mining uncovers thousands of these nearly invisible correlations, and marketing wizards use the results to maximize the store's profits.

But data mining can also be used to spot interesting patterns in other kinds of data. Just by crunching credit card numbers, you could find out that there's some guy in Chicago who's been buying an awful lot of fertilizer—the kind that can be turned into truck bombs. Or someone in New York who does a lot of travel to exotic foreign locales, and who also signs up for courses on how to fly jumbo jets.

Hiawatha Bray, "A Wasted Opportunity in the War on Terror," *Boston.com*, August 15, 2005. Republished with permission of the Boston Globe, conveyed through Pars International Corp. www.boston.com.

According to *The New York Times*, a secret Pentagon program called Able Danger used data-mining technology to determine that Atta and three of his 9/11 buddies were probably members of an Al Qaeda murder cell on US soil. If true, it's an impressive piece of detective work. And the data miners might be capable of even more remarkable feats, if only our government hadn't wasted the past two years.

In 2003, members of Congress of both parties shut down an experimental military research program called Terrorism Information Awareness. Originally known as Total Information Awareness, or TIA, the program was run by Admiral John Poindexter, best known for his felony conviction—later overturned—in the Iran-Contra scandal [a scandal during the presidency of Ronald Reagan].

TIA was an experimental effort run by the same military research agency that led the development of the Internet. This time, the goal was to develop technologies that would search hundreds of government and commercial databases, in search of patterns that might indicate criminal or terrorist activity.

Note the word "experimental." TIA was nowhere near ready for actual use. Poindexter and company wanted to use made-up data that resembled the stuff in real-world databases. The data would be seeded with subtle hints of suspicious activity, based on actual terrorism incidents. TIA would try to develop technologies that would spot the patterns and sound the alarm.

The mere idea of TIA [Terrorism Information Awareness] horrified civil libertarians right across the political spectrum.

But the mere idea of TIA horrified civil libertarians right across the political spectrum. Former *New York Times* columnist William Safire led the way, claiming that Poindexter wanted to create dossiers on every American—an absurdly inaccurate description of the project. But no matter. The resulting firestorm led to the shutdown of the project and to Poindexter's resignation.

These days, Poindexter spends his days sailing on Chesapeake Bay. He doubts that data mining alone could have rolled up the 9/11 terror network. "It was only after the fact that the significance of this particular group was seen as important," he said. Still, Poindexter believes that if Able Danger information had been shared with other law enforcement entities, it might have made a difference. "There may very well have been other evidence that would have made the group stand out," he said. The advanced techniques he'd tried to develop might have enabled even better information analysis, and better sharing of data between law enforcement agencies. "I do think that cancellation of the TIA programs did weaken the nation's security," said Poindexter.

Maybe he exaggerates. Some computer industry experts doubt that TIA could ever have worked. "I thought it was a harebrained scheme," said Richard Smith, a computer security expert and former head of the Privacy Foundation. Smith doubts press reports that the Able Danger team used data mining to spot Atta. "It was simple spy work that identified these people," he said.

Smart, aggressive use of computer technology could help us spot . . . [potential terrorists] before it's too late.

Smith is biased, in an admirable way. He's horrified, with good reason, by TIA's potential to invade our privacy. But it's scarcely rational to ban the program outright, like outlawing telephones because they can be tapped. Instead, programs like TIA should have continued, on an experimental basis. Its developers were already testing ways to build privacy into this system. For instance, you can analyze credit card purchases without knowing the names of the cardholders.

Meanwhile, Congress could have calmed down and set sensible restrictions on the system's real-world use. Suppose TIA's anonymous credit card analysis spots something hinky, and the cops want a name and address. We might let them have the info, but only if a federal judge agrees. By now, TIA researchers would have two more years of know-how under their belts. And lawmakers could have crafted strong but flexible statutes to prevent abuses. Instead, federal data-mining projects continue, but they're buried inside the "black" budgets of our various spy agencies. Here it will be even harder to ride herd on the projects—and harder to ensure evidence of an impending attack is shared with cops on the front lines.

It's possible—likely, even—that another Mohammed Atta is already in place, rehearsing for the next nightmare. . . . Smart, aggressive use of computer technology could help us spot him before it's too late.

The Protect America Act Modernizes America's Foreign Surveillance Capabilities

George W. Bush

George W. Bush was the 43rd president of the United States (2000–2008).

Every day, our intelligence, law enforcement and homeland security professionals confront enemies who are smart, who are ruthless, and who are determined to murder innocent people to achieve their objectives. It is the job of Congress to give the professionals the tools they need to do their work as effectively as possible.

The Importance of FISA

You don't have to worry about the motivation of the people out here; what we do have to worry about is to make sure that they have all the tools they need to do their job. One of the most important tools they use is the Foreign Intelligence Surveillance Act, or FISA. The law provides a critical legal foundation that allows our intelligence community to monitor terrorist communications while protecting the freedoms of American people. Unfortunately, the law is dangerously out of date.

When FISA was passed nearly 30 years ago, the legal protections were based on differences in the way that domestic and overseas communications were transmitted. New technologies have come into being since the law was written. Technologies like the disposable cell phone or the Internet eliminated many of those differences. So one of the consequences of the way the law was originally drafted is that when

George W. Bush, "President Bush Discusses the Protect America Act of 2007," www
.whitehouse.gov, September 19, 2007.

technology changed, legal protections meant only for the people in the United States began applying to terrorists on foreign soil. As a result, our intelligence professionals reported that they were missing a significant amount of real-time intelligence needed to protect the American people. So earlier this year [National Security Agency] Director [Admiral Mike] McConnell sent Congress legislation to fix the problem.

[The Protect America Act] . . . has helped close a critical intelligence gap, allowing us to collect important foreign intelligence and information about terrorist plots.

The Protect America Act

In August [2007], a bipartisan majority in Congress passed the Protect America Act. This law has helped close a critical intelligence gap, allowing us to collect important foreign intelligence and information about terrorist plots. The problem is the law expires on February 1st—that's 135 days from today. The threat from al Qaeda is not going to expire in 135 days.

So I call on Congress to make the Protect America Act permanent. The need for action is clear. Director McConnell has warned that unless the FISA reforms in the Act are made permanent, our national security professionals will lose critical tools they need to protect our country. Without these tools, it'll be harder to figure out what our enemies are doing to train, recruit and infiltrate operatives in our country. Without these tools our country will be much more vulnerable to attack.

Unfortunately, some in Congress now want to restrict the tools. These restrictions would impede the flow of information that helps us protect our people. These restrictions would reopen gaps in our intelligence that we had just closed. As I did in August, in evaluating any FISA bill, I will ask Director McConnell whether the legislation gives him what he needs to protect our nation. The question I'm going to ask is, do our professionals have the tools necessary to do the job to protect the American people from further attack?

Liability Protection

In addition to making the Protect America Act permanent, I urge Congress to take up other critical proposals included in the comprehensive FISA reform my administration submitted last April. It's particularly important for Congress to provide meaningful liability protection to those companies now facing multi-billion dollar lawsuits only because they are believed to have assisted in efforts to defend our nation following the 9/11 attacks. Additionally, without this protection, state secrets could be revealed in connection with those lawsuits—and our ability to protect our people would be weakened.

At stake in this debate is more than a piece of legislation. The decisions Congress makes will directly affect our ability to save American lives. I look forward to working with Congress to enact this legislation as quickly as possible, so that our intelligence officials will continue to have the tools they need to keep the American people safe.

Organizations to Contact

The editors have compiled the following list of organizations concerned with the issues debated in this book. The descriptions are derived from materials provided by the organizations. All have publications or information available for interested readers. The list was compiled on the date of publication of the present volume; the information provided here may change. Readers need to remember that many organizations take several weeks or longer to respond to inquiries.

American Civil Liberties Union (ACLU)
125 Broad St., 18th Floor, New York, NY   10004-2400
(212) 549-2500
e-mail: aclu@aclu.org
Web site: www.aclu.org

The ALCU is a national organization that works to defend Americans' civil rights guaranteed by the U.S. Constitution, arguing that measures to protect national security should not compromise fundamental civil liberties. It publishes and distributes policy statements, pamphlets, and press releases with titles such as "In Defense of Freedom in a Time of Crisis" and "National ID Cards: 5 Reasons Why They Should Be Rejected."

American Enterprise Institute (AEI)
1150 17th St. NW, Washington, DC   20036
(202) 862-5800
Web site: www.aei.org

The AEI for Public Policy Research is a scholarly research institute dedicated to preserving limited government, private enterprise, and a strong foreign policy and national defense. It publishes books, including *Study of Revenge: The First World Trade Center Attack and Saddam Hussein's War Against America*. Articles about terrorism and September 11 can be found in its magazine, *American Enterprise*, and on its Web site.

The Brookings Institution

1775 Massachusetts Ave. NW, Washington, DC 20036
(202) 797-6000 • fax: (202) 797-6004
e-mail: brookinfo@brook.edu
Web site: www.brookings.org

The Brookings Institution, founded in 1927, is a think tank that conducts research and education in foreign policy, economics, government, and the social sciences. In 2001, it began America's Response to Terrorism, a project that provides briefings and analysis to the public and is featured on the center's Web site. Other publications include the quarterly *Brookings Review*, periodic *Policy Briefs*, and such books as *Terrorism and U.S. Foreign Policy*.

Cato Institute

1000 Massachusetts Ave. NW, Washington, DC 20001-5403
(202) 842-0200 • fax: (202) 842-3490
e-mail: cato@cato.org
Web site: www.cato.org

The Cato Institute is a nonpartisan public policy research foundation dedicated to limiting the role of government and protecting individual liberties. It publishes the quarterly magazine *Regulation*, the bimonthly *Cato Policy Report*, and numerous policy papers and articles. Works on terrorism include "Does U.S. Intervention Overseas Breed Terrorism?" and "Military Tribunals No Answer."

Center for Defense Information

1779 Massachusetts Ave. NW, Suite 615
Washington, DC 20036
(202) 332-0600 • fax: (202) 462-4559
e-mail: info@cdi.org
Web site: www.cdi.org

The Center for Defense Information is a nonpartisan, nonprofit organization that researches all aspects of global security. It seeks to educate the public and policymakers about such issues as weapons systems, security policy, and defense budgeting. Publications include the monthly *Defense Monitor*, the issue brief "National Missile Defense: What Does It All Mean?," and the studies "Homeland Security: A Competitive Strategies Approach" and "Reforging the Sword."

Center for Immigration Studies

1522 K St. NW, Suite 820, Washington, DC   20005-1202
(202) 466-8185 • fax (202) 466-8076
e-mail: center@cis.org
Web site: www.cis.org

The Center for Immigration Studies, the nation's only think tank dedicated to research and analysis of the economic, social, and demographic impacts of immigration on the United States, is an independent, nonpartisan, nonprofit research organization founded in 1985. The center aims to expand public support for an immigration policy that is both pro-immigrant and low-immigration. Among its publications are "The USA PATRIOT Act of 2001: A Summary of the Anti-Terrorism Law's Immigration-Related Provisions" and "America's Identity Crisis: Document Fraud Is Pervasive and Pernicious."

Center for Security Policy (CSP)

1920 L St. NW, Suite 210, Washington, DC   20036
(202) 835-9077
e-mail: info@centerforsecuritypolicy.org
Web site: www.centerforsecuritypolicy.org

CSP is a nonprofit organization that informs the debate and ensures effective action on vital national security issues. CSP believes America should have a strong national defense and should promote security through military, economic, and diplomatic means. The organization's Web site details several CSP projects relating to terrorism, Middle East policy, energy security, and national defense.

Center for Strategic & International Studies (CSIS)
1800 K St. NW, Washington, DC   20006
(202) 887-0200 • fax: (202) 775-3199
email: aschwartz@csis.org
Web site: www.csis.org

The (CSIS) is a nonprofit public policy think tank based in Washington, D.C., that focuses on foreign policy issues. CSIS's Web site includes a page entitled "Homeland Security," which contains in-depth policy reports, testimony, and news about homeland security issues.

Central Intelligence Agency (CIA)
Office of Public Affairs, Washington, DC   20505
(703) 482-0623 • fax: (703) 482-1739
Web site: www.cia.gov

The CIA coordinates national intelligence gathering and analysis impacting U.S. security. The CIA is an independent agency, responsible to the president and accountable to the American people through the Intelligence Oversight Committee of the U.S. Congress. The CIA publishes a *Factbook on Intelligence* and other reports that are available on its Web site.

Chemical and Biological Arms Control Institute (CBACI)
1747 Pennsylvania Ave. NW, 7th Floor
Washington, DC   20006
(202) 296-3550 • fax: (202) 296-3574
e-mail: cbaci@cbaci.org

CBACI is a nonprofit corporation that promotes arms control and nonproliferation, with particular focus on the elimination of chemical and biological weapons. It draws on an extensive international network to provide research, analysis, technical support, and education in the areas of arms control and nonproliferation. The institute publishes the bimonthly report *Dispatch*, as well as "Bioterrorism in the United States: Threat, Preparedness, and Response" and "Contagion and Conflict: Health as a Global Security Challenge."

Federal Aviation Administration (FAA)

800 Independence Ave. SW, Washington, DC   20591
(800) 322-7873 • fax: (202) 267-3484
Web site: www.faa.gov

The FAA is part of the U.S. Department of Transportation. Its primary responsibility is regulating civil aviation to promote safety and fulfill the requirements of national defense. Among its publications are *Technology Against Terrorism, Air Piracy, Airport Security, and International Terrorism: Winning the War Against Hijackers* and *Security Tips for Air Travelers.*

Federal Bureau of Investigation (FBI)

935 Pennsylvania Ave. NW, Room 7972
Washington, DC   20535
(202) 324-3000
Web site: www.fbi.gov

The FBI, the principle investigative arm of the U.S. Department of Justice, investigates and prosecutes federal crimes. It is also responsible for countering terrorism and gathering foreign intelligence on U.S. soil. The FBI is often called upon to aid other law enforcement bodies at the federal, state, and local levels. Speeches, press releases, and other issue papers pertaining to FBI activities are available on its Web site.

The Heritage Foundation

214 Massachusetts Ave. NE, Washington, DC   20002-4999
(202) 546-4400 • fax (202) 546-8328
e-mail: info@heritage.org
Web site: www.heritage.org

The Heritage Foundation, a conservative organization, provides research and information on current public policies. The institute has supported the deployment of troops to Iraq and other presidential initiatives concerning the U.S. war on terror. The Heritage Foundation Web site provides numerous online publications analyzing national security and other areas of government policy.

Institute for Policy Studies (IPS)

733 15th St. NW, Suite 1020, Washington, DC   20005
(202) 234-9382 • fax (202) 387-7915
Web site: www.ips-dc.org

The IPS is a progressive think tank that works to develop societies built on the values of justice and nonviolence. It publishes reports, such as *Global Perspectives: A Media Guide to Foreign Policy Experts*. Numerous articles and interviews on September 11 and terrorism are available on its Web site.

National Security Agency (NSA)

9800 Savage Road, Ft. Meade, MD   20755-6248
(301) 688-6524
Web site: www.nsa.gov

The NSA coordinates, directs, and performs activities, such as designing cipher systems, that protect American information systems and produce foreign intelligence information. It is the largest employer of mathematicians in the United States and also hires the nation's best codemakers and codebreakers. Speeches, briefings, and reports are available at the agency's Web site.

RAND Corporation

1776 Main St., PO Box 2138, Santa Monica, CA   90407-2138
(310) 393-0411 • fax: (310) 393-4818
Web site: www.rand.org

The RAND Corporation is a nonprofit institution that helps improve policy and decision-making through research and analysis. The corporation has studied terrorism for thirty years and has published numerous books on the subject, as well as on foreign policy and national security. Research papers on these topics are also available on the RAND Web site.

U.S. Department of Homeland Security (DHS)
Washington, DC 20528
(202) 282-8000
Web site: www.dhs.gov

Created shortly after the September 11, 2001, terrorist attacks, DHS was envisioned as a central agency that could coordinate federal, state, and local resources to prevent or respond to threats to the American homeland. The department contains many subdivisions that deal specifically with trade, immigration, preparedness, and research. The DHS Web site contains speeches and Congressional testimony by DHS representatives, as well as mission statements and department performance records.

U.S. Department of State, Counterterrorism Office
Office of Public Affairs, Room 2507, Washington, DC 20520
(202) 647-4000
e-mail: secretary@state.gov
Web site: www.state.gov

The office works to develop and implement American counterterrorism strategy and to improve cooperation with foreign governments. Articles and speeches by government officials are available at its Web site.

Washington Institute for Near East Policy
1828 L St. NW, Suite 1050, Washington, DC 20036
(202) 452-0650 • fax: (202) 223-5364
e-mail: info@washingtoninstitute.org
Web site: www.washingtoninstitute.org

The institute is an independent organization that produces research and analysis on the Middle East and U.S. policy in the region. It publishes position papers and reports on Middle Eastern politics and social developments. It also publishes position papers on Middle Eastern military issues and U.S. policy, including "The Future of Iraq" and "Building for Peace: An American Strategy for the Middle East."

Bibliography

Books

Joseph Biden and William C. Nicholson — *Homeland Security Law And Policy.* Springfield, IL: Charles C. Thomas Publisher, 2005.

Cynthia Brown, ed. — *Lost Liberties: Ashcroft and the Assault on Personal Freedom.* New York: The New Press, 2003.

Jane Bullock and George Haddow — *Introduction to Homeland Security.* Oxford, UK: Butterworth-Heinemann, 2006.

David Cole and Jules Lobel — *Less Safe, Less Free: Why America Is Losing the War on Terror.* New York: New Press, 2007.

Christopher Cooper and Robert Block — *Disaster: Hurricane Katrina and the Failure of Homeland Security.* New York: Times Books, 2006.

Ted Gottfried — *Homeland Security vs. Constitutional Rights.* Kirkland, WA: 21st Century 2003.

Arthur S. Hulnick — *Keeping Us Safe: Secret Intelligence and Homeland Security.* New York: Praeger Publishers, 2004.

Thomas McInerney and Paul E. Vallely — *Endgame: The Blueprint for Victory in the War on Terror.* Washington, DC: Regnery Publishing, 2006.

Richard Miniter   *Shadow War: The Untold Story of How Bush Is Winning the War on Terror*. Washington, DC: Regnery Publishing, 2004.

Charles Perrow   *The Next Catastrophe: Reducing Our Vulnerabilities to Natural, Industrial, and Terrorist Disasters*. Princeton, NJ: Princeton University Press, 2007.

Marcus Ranum   *The Myth of Homeland Security*. Indianapolis, IN: Wiley, 2003.

Mark Sauter and   *Homeland Security: A Complete Guide*
James Carafano   *to Understanding, Preventing and Surviving Terrorism*. New York: McGraw-Hill, 2005.

Bruce Schneier   *Beyond Fear*. New York: Springer, 2003.

Jonathan R.   *Terrorism and Homeland Security:*
White   *An Introduction*. Belmont, CA: Wadsworth Publishing, 2008.

Periodicals

Airport Security   "DHS Increases Funding for REAL
Report   ID Grant Program," February 13, 2008.

The Atlantic   "Money for Nothing," October 2007,
Monthly   p. 30.

Joseph Bonney   "Holes in the DHS," *The Journal of Commerce*, October 1, 2007, p. 6.

George Bruno "Look Out for the Next Homeland Security Mess," *New Hampshire Business Review*, September 28, 2007, p. 21.

Wilson P. Dizard "Study: Flaws in Fusion Centers: Thompson Says DHS-Backed Centers Are Falling Short of Their Mission," *Government Computer News*, July 30, 2007, p. 5.

Robert Dreyfuss "There Is No War on Terror," *TomPaine.com*, September 13, 2006. www.tompaine.com/articles/2006/09/13/there_is_no_war_on_terror.php.

R.G. Edmonson "GAO Report Gives DHS Failing Grades," *Shipping Digest*, October 1, 2007.

R.G. Edmonson "Ridge Looks Back, Forward," *The Journal of Commerce*, October 15, 2007, p. 25.

Sandra I. Erwin "Homeland Security Policies Overlook Essential Issues, Says Shipping Executive," *National Defense*, November 2007, p. 20.

William Fisher "Civil Libertarians Warn of 'PATRIOT Act Lite,'" *Inter Press Service*, November 28, 2007. www.antiwar.com/ips/fisher.php?articleid=11968.

Florida Shipper "Streamline Congressional Oversight of DHS, Chertoff Says," January 21, 2008.

Kelly Holman   "Cyber Terror Threat Looms: Financial Industry Infrastructure Still at Risk, Group Says," *Investment Dealers' Digest*, February 4, 2008.

Mark Hosenball and Michael Isikoff   "A Sense of Unease; Al Qaeda's Regrouped. But What Does that Mean?," *Newsweek*, July 23, 2007, p. 36.

Elaine Kamarck   "Fixing the Department of Homeland Security," *Progressive Policy Institute*, November 14, 2007. www.ppionline.org/ppi_ci.cfm? contentid=254508&knlgAreaID=124 &subsecid=900019.

Rachael King   "Homeland Insecurity: The Homeland Security Dept.'s Overreliance on Outside Contractors and Insufficient Management of Them Could Leave the U.S. Vulnerable," *Business Week Online*, December 18, 2007. www.businessweek.com/technology/ content/dec2007/tc20071214_5673 70.htm.

Rachael King   "Is Homeland Security Too Focused on Now? The Department's Projects Emphasize Near-Term Results. But Some Say that Could Leave the U.S. Vulnerable to Threats that Can't Be Anticipated," *Business Week Online*, December 20, 2007. www.businessweek.com/technology/ content/dec2007/tc20071219_6959 82.htm.

Elliot C. McLaughlin   "Federal ID Plan Raises Privacy Concerns," *CNN*, August 16, 2007. www.cnn.com/2007/POLITICS/08/16/real.id/index.html.

Robert L. Mitchell   "Big Brother Really Is Watching: Homeland Security Is Bankrolling Futuristic Technology to Nab Terrorists Before They Strike," *Computerworld*, January 14, 2008, p. 22.

Amanda Ripley   "We've Come Undone," *Time*, August 20, 2007, p. 38.

Steven E. Roberts   "Maritime Workers and Homeland Security," *Miami Daily Business Review*, August 27, 2007.

Matthew Robinson   "Civil Liberties and the War on Terror: An Eight Part Series," Appalachian State University, October 31, 2006. www.justiceblind.com/usapatriotactseries.htm.

Bruce Schneier   "We're Giving Up Privacy and Getting Little in Return: Better to Put People, Not Computers, in Charge of Investigating Potential Plots," *Minneapolis Star Tribune*, May 31, 2006. www.schneier.com/essay-115.html.

Matthew Swibel and Brian Wingfield   "Scary Symptoms," *Forbes*, December 10, 2007, p. 44.

Index